RACE SKILLS
for Alpine Skiing

By Ellen Post Foster

Photography by Alan Schönberger

RACE SKILLS
for Alpine Skiing

By Ellen Post Foster

Copyright © 1994 Turning Point Ski Foundation

5 4 3 2 1

All rights reserved. No part of this publication may be reproduced or transmitted in any form or any means, electronic or mechanical, including photography, recording or any other information storage and retrieval system, without prior permission in writing from the publisher.

Published in the United States in 1994 by the Turning Point Ski Foundation, P.O. Box 246, South Hero, VT 05486

Designed by Alan Schönberger

Books available from the Turning Point Ski Foundation, P.O. Box 943, Edwards, CO 81632

Printed and bound in Harrisonburg, VA, by RR Donnelley & Sons Company
Color separation by RR Donnelley & Sons Company

It was very windy. The racer turned toward the ski lift as her team mates entered the lodge to get warm. As she rode the lift alone, she seemed to concentrate with intense determination. Alone at the top of the course, she stepped into the start and studied the gates. Although all sound was muffled by wind, she could hear in her mind the chants of spectators. Louder now, and clearly, came the signal. Leaping from the start, she plunged down the course. The wind was behind her, as if encouraging her furious descent. She could almost feel the clamor of the crowd, cheering her on. She only cared about racing from gate to gate, as though that, in itself, was the goal. She crossed the finish, raising her arms in victory. The World Cup accompaniment stayed on the wind and faded far away as she slid to a standstill. "One day..." she whispered to the wind.

Ellen Post Foster

Where Dreams Begin

ACKNOWLEDGMENTS

In years to come, I'll remember three summers of writing books. I'll think of an island in Vermont at the end of those summers, where Alan Schönberger devoted his days and nights to turning my manuscripts into books. Tirelessly, he developed film, wrote revisions and printed pages. At those times, I learned so much. Just as a coach encourages an athlete to challenge her potential, Alan prompted me to do my best work. Thank you, Alan, for making my dream a reality.

I would like to express heartfelt thanks: To my mother and father, Frieda and Dan Post. My father spent countless hours diligently helping me through revisions; to Werner Schnydrig, an extraordinary coach with whom I have discussed ski racing and shared ideals for sixteen years; to Emily Katz Anhalt, my skiing friend since childhood who carefully edits my writings from the perspective of an English professor; to JP Peppler, Dave Galusha, Carol Levine, Betty Gras, Scott Nyman, Dee Byrne, and Ed Cohen, who reviewed my work with care.

I would like to express my gratitude to Mike DeCesaro for his contribution on behalf of Skis Dynastar, and to Marc Hauser and Dennis Leedom for their contribution on behalf of MPH Associates, Inc and Boeri Ski Helmets. Their belief in my work has made this book possible.

I greatly appreciate the vote of confidence I received from the members of the Professional Ski Instructors of America–Rocky Mountain division's Education Foundation. I am grateful for their support, and to have the opportunity to share my knowledge as an instructor and coach with the members of my profession.

Thank you to Alan Henceroth and the Arapahoe Basin Ski Patrol for their proficiency and endless support which has enabled us to have many successful photographic sessions.

Once again, Brad, Randi and Will Foster have provided the understanding and support that has allowed me to write this book.

Turning Point Ski Foundation The *Turning Point Ski Foundation* is a non-profit organization that develops and publishes educational materials to help young skiers achieve their goals. Books, such as *Race Skills for Alpine Skiing*, are designed to enrich skiers' experiences as they strive for excellence.

Alan Schönberger Ski Bum The theatrical stage production, "Alan Schönberger Ski Bum in *Piano Roll*", is the flagship fundraiser of the *Turning Point Ski Foundation*. Performance artist, Alan Schönberger, combines the skills and charm of the European circus with the surreal image of figure skiing as he skis on stage. The performance captures the essence of our sport. It teaches us that simple things are beautiful, that technology must have heart, and that dreams can come true if we face the challenges.

FOREWORD

Bill Egan
Head Men's 'Speed' Coach
United States Ski Team

This book is a must for all coaches and serious ski racers and for anyone who aspires to be one. It is extremely well written, thorough, and professional, and it will increase the ability and enjoyment of every racing enthusiast.

Foster draws on her impressive background in ski teaching and coaching to produce thorough and accurate descriptions of technique and tactics. These descriptions are simple and easily understood—an unusual feature in a book of this sort. The book also contains invaluable exercises for obtaining the tactical and technical skills necessary for success. This is something most ski racing books don't provide.

Foster clarifies ski teaching and ski coaching jargon and establishes a common ground for professionals and participants who seek to make the sport a more dynamic, more safe, life-long activity. This is a very much needed source of information for both racers and coaches. It is more accessible for a wider range of readers than any skiing book I have read. This is a book I will have all of my athletes and coaches read.

Mike Porter
National Demonstration Team Head Coach,
Professional Ski Instructors of America

This book presents the most well-rounded approach to ski racing that I have seen. It is essential reading for coaches, instructors and developing athletes. The book is systematic, logical, and clear. Using very specific, easily understood exercises, Foster enlivens highly complex subject matter. She has an impressive ability to isolate the key skills and ingredients in a clear, concise manner. She creates a specific and practical exercise line for each topic she is developing. This is extremely refreshing. The reader absorbs the theory and obtains the necessary reinforcement by means of the tasks Foster sets up. Even the most seasoned coach will gain new ideas and exercises to improve his or her coaching effectiveness. Coaches and athletes will find this a treasure trove.

Lester Keller
Western Region Alpine Director,
United States Skiing

In the fall of 1992, I took a job as the Alpine Program Director and Head Coach of the Winter Park Ski Club, a long-established organization. At the time, the staff's goal was to redirect the club's focus and energy toward high quality racing experiences for their young skiers. At first, I thought this would prove to be a long and arduous process that could only be accomplished after several years of great effort. With mixed feelings, I set about the chore.

In one of the most fortunate occurrences of the first year, Ellen, a returning member of the under-fourteen coaching staff, stepped into a leadership void in that group. By the New Year, she had agreed to be Age Class Head Coach. We never looked back. Ellen's experience as an instructor and elite competitor, combined with her constant quest for knowledge, brought the racers to unprecedented levels in their development and application of new skills.

Over the next five years, our "Age Class" team reaped the benefits of Ellen's leadership, knowledge, understanding, and care. Most made great technical progress. Some had great results. Some won many ski races. But most importantly, all were given the best opportunity to progress, in all dimensions of athletics, in a way that made coming to training a joy and their team a central part of their life.

Race Skills for Alpine Skiing reflects the same commitment to providing useful, practical information to coaches and athletes. It is a clear presentation of immediately applicable technical drills that follow logically from technical and tactical descriptions in all alpine disciplines.

This work can be studied and used over and over. It will serve as both a stand-alone coach's reference book and an important addition to any serious library on ski and racing instruction.

PREFACE

Tommy Moe
1994 Olympic Downhill champion

Coaching played a major role in my development. My coaches have always been there for me and encouraged me to push harder. The importance of a good coach doesn't diminish through the years. A coach needs to really understand the technical and tactical aspects of ski racing. The information contained in this book will be very helpful for coaches/instructors, skiers, and parents. A coach is not only a leader but a person who teaches skiing so that it includes the element of fun. Ellen's approach to skill development in this book and in the *Alpine Skills Achievement Manual* makes learning an exciting experience.

A young skier must gradually work up to skiing at high speeds. For instance, a skier should establish a good technique in Giant Slalom before tackling Downhill. *Race Skills for Alpine Skiing* starts with Giant Slalom turns and develops the skills that are necessary for the speed events. Anyone can ski down a well groomed slope on a sunny day. But it takes a good skier to be able to adjust to crusty snow or icy conditions. Learning to adapt to varying conditions sharpens a skiers skills and will allow her/him to improve technically. Ellen's work is based on a strong foundation that applies technically correct skills to the demands of ski racing.

Skiing has provided me with the opportunity to travel around the world, meet interesting people, represent my country in two Olympic competitions, and do what I love the most—carving turns down white slopes. *Race Skills for Alpine Skiing* will help racers achieve what is most important to them. I commend the Turning Point Ski Foundation for this contribution to ski racing.

INTRODUCTION

Ellen Post Foster

I've often thought that new experiences were as much for coaches as for their students. Learning was as important in my job as teaching. One could always learn from other professionals, parents, situations, and of course from the racers.

My first experiences as a Downhill coach are still clear in my mind because I had so much to learn. I distinctly remember my feelings upon hearing that I would be in charge of our junior team during an upcoming race. I thought my experience was too limited to fulfill this responsibility. I also remember our head coach was surprised at my concern. At first, he did not take it seriously. I asked for paper, pencil and a description of the course. Question followed question until they were no longer necessary. *My* coach spoke at length and in detail. Perhaps he remembered his first Downhill experience.

That evening, I drew the course from his description. I copied notes into my notebook and wrote a plan.

In the weeks to come, I asked to assist at an "ability class" race and was assigned a section of the course to observe. Taking careful notes, I studied our racers and compared their performance to that of the fastest competitors. I listened to coaches comment on other sections of the course and during course inspection–and added to my notebook.

As the skills of my racers developed, and they learned from new adventures, my notebook expanded. Eventually it was replaced with a new notebook, containing new names and new experiences. Last spring, I took the former notebook from my shelf and turned the pages. I held in my hands a great amount of information that would help other coaches. I realized how much I had at one time desired a book to provide answers to my questions and lend direction for my coaching.

Over the years, I have had many wonderful opportunities to learn from great coaches. *Race Skills for Alpine Skiing* is filled with this information. The material is organized for coaches, instructors, racers, and parents to use. Although I tend to picture young skiers, I think readers will find this material to be pertinent for skiers of all ages. The strengths and weaknesses of the young skiers I have coached have never seemed different from those of adults.

There are six chapters in *Race Skills for Alpine Skiing*:

- Chapter 1 Turn Technique
- Chapter 2 Slalom
- Chapter 3 Giant Slalom
- Chapter 4 Super-G and Downhill
- Chapter 5 Equipment
- Chapter 6 Race Procedure

The description in Chapter 1, *Turn Technique*, is based on the mechanics of a Giant Slalom turn. This chapter contains an explanation of carved turns, a description of body movement and ski action, and a list of turn characteristics. *Turn Technique* concludes with examples of how the intensity, duration, and timing of movements determine the size, shape, and speed of turns.

The Giant Slalom, Slalom, and speed events (Super-G and Downhill) chapters are subdivided into five topics. The content is designed to teach and refine skills that are necessary for racing.

- Technique
- Skill Development
- Gate Drills
- Course Description
- Tactics

Technique covers information that is unique to each discipline. For example, Downhill tuck position and methods for clearing Slalom poles are addressed in this section, in their respective chapters.

The exercises in *Skill Development* are designed to enhance race performance through the development of technique.

The *Gate Drills* section features drills that develop both technical and tactical skills. These drills center around short-length courses that allow racers to focus strongly on specific themes.

In the *Course Description* segment, many diagrams illustrate gate dimensions, gate combinations and course layouts. Activities, such as the *Paper Cup Slalom* and *Course Drawing*, are included for skiers to understand better the components of a race course.

The information provided under *Tactics* explains the racer's line through a course. It also suggests ways to teach tactics and describes a method for course inspection. The Slalom section, in particular, is filled with photographs that show the layout of different gate combinations along with the racer's position in relation to the gates.

Chapter five, *Equipment*, includes information about ski length for the speed events, protective gear for Slalom and Giant Slalom, and a look at ski helmets for all events.

The last chapter, *Race Procedure*, pertains to course setting, start and finish procedure, and selected rules that coaches and racers should know.

Following the last chapter is a *Glossary* of terms that enables readers to locate definitions easily. The *Appendix* provides an in-depth perspective regarding the importance of ski helmets.

Race Skills for Alpine Skiing is the third book in a series produced by the *Turning Point Ski Foundation*. This non-profit organization is dedicated to helping the youth of our sport. It publishes educational material to assist ski professionals, parents, and participants. The *Alpine Skills Achievement Manual*, the first book produced by the foundation, emphasizes skill development maneuvers that build well-rounded skiing skills. It can be used in conjunction with this book to prepare skiers for the technical demands of racing. In future printings, this book will be renamed *Technical Skills for Alpine Skiing*. The information in the second book, *Conditioning Skills for Alpine Skiing*, can be used to prepare skiers for the physical demands of ski racing. It includes dry-land and on-the-snow conditioning exercises.

Following are some thoughts to keep in mind when using the information on the upcoming pages.

- Directed free-skiing is a very important part of race training. The mountain provides the optimal environment for skiers to learn technique and apply their skills to the demands of terrain and snow conditions. "Directed" refers to skiing with technical goals in mind. These objectives come from the coach, and later from within the racer as well. Athletes should strive to be the best *skiers* they can be. Only then, will competitive success follow.

• Encourage athletes to learn from every opportunity. Find the positive aspect of every effort.

• Vary the focus to develop well-rounded skills. Place the emphasis on tactics following a technical run. Then, have skiers concentrate on racing as fast as they possibly can.

• Encourage precision and accuracy while free-skiing or practicing exercises to maximize their effectiveness.

• Practice in different weather and snow conditions to be ready for all race situations.

• Encourage a love for skiing.

When I page through my old notebook, I remember the moments, the racers, their expectations, their successes, their hopes, their dreams. I think back to the time I skied alone on a windy day.

This book is dedicated to every racer and coach who has a dream.

SYNOPSIS

CHAPTER 1 **TURN TECHNIQUE**
CHAPTER 2 **GIANT SLALOM**
CHAPTER 3 **SLALOM**
CHAPTER 4 **SUPER-G AND DOWNHILL**
CHAPTER 5 **EQUIPMENT**
CHAPTER 6 **RACE PROCEDURE**

GLOSSARY
APPENDIX
BIBLIOGRAPHY

DEMONSTRATORS:

Onie Bolduc, age 12
David Lamb, age 11
Christopher Malato, age 14

Tyson Bolduc, age 10
Liz Golting, age 10
Michael Nyman, age 13
Steven Nyman, age 12

Ellen Post Foster
Scott Nyman

CONTENTS

Acknowledgments
Foreword by Bill Egan, Mike Porter and Lester Keller
Preface by Tommy Moe
Introduction
Synopsis

RACE SKILLS for Alpine Skiing

1   CHAPTER 1 **TURN TECHNIQUE**

3   **Carved Turns**
4   **Turn Description**
5   **Characteristics**
6   **Turn Shape**
6   **Speed Play**

CHAPTER 2 **GIANT SLALOM**

TECHNIQUE

SKILL DEVELOPMENT

11   **Carved Wedge Turns**
12   **Upper Body Position**
12   **Wedge/Parallel**
13   **Partner Wedge with Slalom Poles**
13   **Javelin Turns**
13   **Slow Speed Turns**
14   **Different Turn Shapes**
14   **Pole Plant**

CHAPTER 2 (Continued) GIANT SLALOM

GATE DRILLS

- 14 Cross-Pole Drill
- 15 Creating Courses
- 16 Intermittent Gate Series
- 16 One Ski Pole
- 16 No Ski Poles

COURSE DESCRIPTION

- 17 Open, Closed, Oblique Gate Dimensions
- 18 Delay Combination
- 18 Course Diagram
- 18 Giant Slalom Worksheet
- 18 Course Drawing
- 19 Paper Cup Course
- 19 Racer Set

GIANT SLALOM TACTICS

- 19 Rise Line
- 20 Exit Angle
- 21 Closer Line
- 21 Delay the Turn
- 22 Transition Between Turns
- 22 Helper Poles/Markers
- 24 Delay Combination
- 26 Look Ahead
- 26 Read Terrain
- 26 Mind Set
- 27 Course Inspection

CHAPTER 3 SLALOM

TECHNIQUE

- 31 Upper Body Position
- 31 Ski Pole Action
- 31 Hand Position
- 32 Clearing Flex Poles

SKILL DEVELOPMENT

- 33 Turn Versatility
- 34 Lead/Follow Medley
- 34 Arms Crossed
- 35 Tuck Turns

CHAPTER 3 (Continued) SLALOM

- 35 Synchronized Shadow
- 36 Synchronized Speed Play
- 37 Synchronized Circle
- 38 Line Pull-out
- 38 Hand Position Exercises

GATE DRILLS

- 39 Two Meter Drill
- 39 Foot Placement
- 40 Slalom Pole Clearing Exercises
- 40 Short Courses
- 42 Course Rotation

COURSE DESCRIPTION

- 43 Gate Dimensions
- 44 Description of Combinations
- 45 Course Diagram
- 45 Slalom Worksheet
- 45 Course Drawing
- 46 Paper Cup Slalom
- 46 Racer Set

SLALOM TACTICS

- 46 Rise Line
- 46 Exit Angle
- 47 Hairpin
- 49 Flush
- 50 Delay Combination
- 51 Visual Awareness
- 51 Course Inspection

CHAPTER 4 SUPER-G AND DOWNHILL

TECHNIQUE

- 55 Turn Description
- 56 Body Positions in Turns
- 58 Tuck Positions
- 58 Downhill Pole

SKILL DEVELOPMENT

- 59 Safety Prerequisites
- 61 Adjusting to Longer Skis

CHAPTER 4 (Continued) SUPER-G AND DOWNHILL

61 Ski Pole Action
62 Flat Ski Exercises
62 Tuck Position Exercises
62 Straight Run Tuck Exercises
63 Traverse Exercises
63 Turn Exercises
65 Transitions Between Turns
65 In the Air

DRILLS

66 Terrain Course
67 Course Elements

COURSE DESCRIPTION

67 Terrain Features
68 Gate Dimensions
68 Course Description
69 Course Drawing

SUPER-G AND DOWNHILL TACTICS

70 Tactics
70 Corridor
71 Course Inspection
71 Training Run Strategy

SPEED EVENT SAFETY

72 Readiness Criteria
71 Helmets
73 Free-skiing
73 In the Course
73 Yellow Zone
74 Stopping Safely

CHAPTER 5 EQUIPMENT

SAFETY EQUIPMENT

77 Slalom and Giant Slalom
77 Helmets for All Events

SPEED EVENTS

78 Ski Length
79 Ski Poles

CHAPTER 6 RACE PROCEDURES

START AND FINISH PROCEDURES

- 83 Timing
- 83 Start Command
- 83 Start Position
- 84 Finish Position
- 84 Come to a Stop
- 84 Clear the Finish

COURSE SETTING

- 84 Technical Data
- 85 Course Setter Responsibilities
- 85 Measure Distances
- 85 Ski the Hill
- 86 Open Gates
- 86 Closed Gates
- 86 Oblique Gates
- 86 Rhythm Sections
- 87 Changes in Rhythm
- 87 Changes in Pitch
- 87 Hairpin
- 88 Flush
- 88 Delay Combination
- 88 Giant Slalom Gate Combinations
- 89 Super-G Gate Combination
- 89 End of Course
- 89 Safety Precautions

SELECTED RULES

- 89 Disqualification
- 89 Interference
- 89 Provisional Re-run
- 90 Protests

GLOSSARY OF TERMS

APPENDIX

BIBLIOGRAPHY

CHAPTER 1
TURN TECHNIQUE

CHAPTER 1 **TURN TECHNIQUE**

The racer's quest is for speed, to ski through the course as fast as possible. This involves technique-- how the racer skis, and tactics-- the skier's line through the course. In order to maintain a fast line through turns, the racer's skis must *carve*. A discussion of carving follows, as well as a description of the technical elements it requires.

Carved Turns

It is helpful to distinguish the term, *carving,* from other terms that describe ways to cross the surface of the snow.
- *Slide*—skis travel forward
- *Slip*—skis travel sideways
- *Pivot*—twisting of a flat ski without changing the skier's direction of travel
- *Skid*—a combination of sliding, slipping and pivoting resulting in a turn

Dynamic, medium radius, parallel turns

In *pure carving,* every point along the length of the ski follows the same path along the arc of the turn and there is no skidding. Carving maintains the racer's speed, whereas skidding decreases speed. Pure carving is accomplished by weighting and angulating the ski so that it bends into a circular arc. The edge of the ski moves along a corresponding circular arc to form a sharp curved track in the snow. The radius of the carved turn is determined by the amount of weight and degree of edge angle applied by the skier, and by the stiffness and sidecut of the ski.

In *steering,* an additional torque is applied to change the path of the ski from the path of pure carving. The torque causes a pivoting action, such that steering always adds a skidding motion to the ski. The steering is applied to decrease the radius of an otherwise pure carved turn, that is, to make a tighter turn. The track is no longer a sharp impression of the angulated ski, but rather, it is a broader swath of disturbed snow caused by the skidding action. In Giant Slalom turns, some steering is usually needed at the beginning of a turn while pure carving is desired for the remainder of the turn. In reality, however, pure carving is a perpetual goal whereas some degree of impure carving is actually achieved. When the term *carving* is used by most skiing professionals, they do not demand pure carving, but imply an acceptable (minimal) amount of skidding. Carving is used in that context in this manual, too.

It is better to steer the skis and not pivot them at the onset of the turn. With pivoting, the skier's direction of travel does not change until the edge engages after the pivot. At that moment, the direction of travel changes abruptly, which generates a braking action on the original path. The flow and the speed of the turn is disrupted. In addition, the sideways momentum results in a skidded turn. With steering, the skis are simultaneously turned and tipped onto edges setting up for a smooth arc, with minimal skidding.

Turn Description

The following technical elements lead to smooth, flowing, and efficient, medium radius turns:

Skis are apart in an open stance for balance, stability, and to acquire an edge angle quickly. An open arm position also assists with balancing movements. At the start of the turn, weight is transferred to the outside ski as it is tipped on edge. Both skis are steered into the turn. Edging increases as the outside ski controls the arc of the carved turn. The inside and outside ski are on corresponding edges since active steering of the inside leg/ski accompanies the movements of the outside ski.

It is essential to pass through a centered position at the start of every turn. This critical part of turn initiation positions the skier for the rest of the turn. Subtle balancing movements are used to adjust weight forward to start the turn, in the center through the turn, and slightly back for the completion of the turn. This action originates from a balancing point located near the back of the arch, in front of the heel. It allows pressure to move along the ski, keeping it from building too strongly at any one place. In this way, the ski travels forward through the arc of the turn without braking sideways.

At the completion of the turn, the upper body faces toward the mid-way point of the upcoming arc. The swing of the ski pole aids in directing the upper body into the next turn. The pole touch occurs during the edge change. These movements assist a strong flow of energy that characterizes linked, carved turns.

There are two types of transitions between turns, as illustrated on the next page. In both cases, the center of mass of the body moves along a continuous curvilinear path. The center of mass never darts sideways into a discontinuous (zig-zag) path. In both cases, the legs and skis move from one side of the center of mass to the other. The *cross-over* transition is used between more distant or longer radius turns. In this case, the weighted skis are flattened after the first turn and then angled onto the opposite edges. Minimal steering is used, and the skier's weight holds the ski firmly on the snow. The diagram shows the smooth paths of the center of mass and the skis. The transition from edge to edge is relatively slow, although the skier's speed can be very high. The skier's legs are extended in both turns, but obviously they are angulated to opposite sides. The body crosses over the skis during the transition and professionals call this a *cross-over* (a).

The *cross-under* transition is used between tight, closely linked turns (b). Rebound at the end of the turn abruptly unweights the skis. In this momentarily unweighted transition period, the skier quickly extends his/her legs toward the outside of the next turn to get on the opposite edges immediately. It is a dynamic, forceful action of the legs, while the center of mass of the body flows smoothly into the next turn. The legs quickly move laterally under the body.

A combination of both cross-under and cross-over movement patterns may occur in one transition. Before and after transition moves, it is important to feel the inside edge of the outside foot/ski in order not to "lose" the edge grip and slip or skid sideways.

A Giant Slalom stance allows for great edge angle and *hip angulation* to provide lateral balance. In hip angulation, the upper body stays relatively vertical, with shoulders level, while the lower body is at a slant to the snow. This is a strong position that relies on skeletal alignment from the foot to the hip for support. It also provides more rotational freedom of the upper body allowing *countering* movements (the outside hip is slightly back in relation to the inside hip) to occur with angulation. Together, a countered and hip angulated stance inhibits the ski tail from skidding through the turn completion, and directs the upper body toward the upcoming turn.

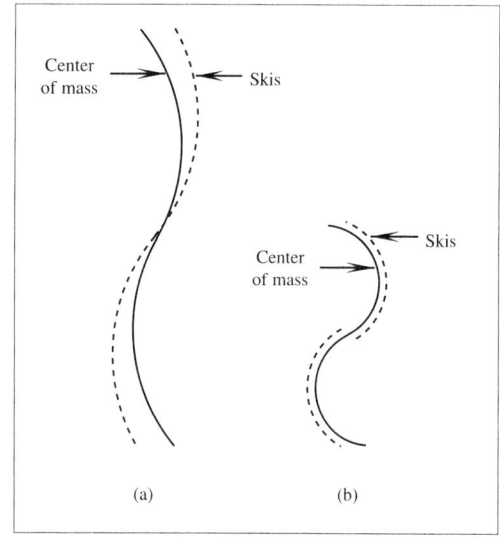

(a) Cross-over transition, (b) Cross-under transition

Characteristics

The coach should look for the following characteristics which are representative of all accurate and precise turns both in and out of a race course:
 a. balanced stance
 b. smooth flow of the skier's center of mass down the hill
 c. balance on the outside ski of the turn
 d. carved, and not skidded turns
 e. steering at the initiation of the turn versus pivoting the skis
 f. a countered, and not rotated position

Characteristics (Continued)

    g. a hip-angulated, and not banked (leaned) position
    h. level shoulders
    i. pole swing and touch
    j. functional body movement versus excessive body moment

Exercises to develop these characteristics can be found in *Technical Skills* for *Alpine Skiing* (formerly *Alpine Skills Achievement Manual*).

Turn Shape

Differently shaped turns result from adjustments in the blending of skills:
    a. Establish the edge early in the turn and ride the edge around, drawing a "C" shape in the snow (a). This turn can occur primarily above or below the gate, or half above and half below, determined by the height above the gate in which this turn is started.
    b. Redirect the skis earlier in the turn to cut through the end of the turn. This requires a high edge angle and pressure very early in the turn. The shape of this turn is similar to a "comma" (b). In relation to turning around a gate, most of the turn occurs above the gate.
    c. Stay longer in the fall line and then concentrate the rotary action later in the turn. In this "J" shaped turn (c), most of the turn occurs after the gate.

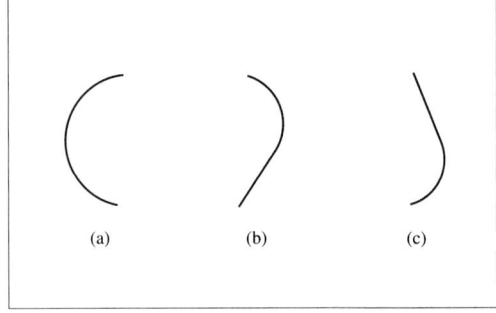

(a) "C" shape, (b) "comma" shape, (c) "J" shape

Speed Play

Racers must be versatile to adjust to any situation in order to maximize every opportunity to increase speed. They have to adapt to the demands of constantly changing terrain and snow conditions as well as a dictated course of descent (race course). The intensity, duration, and timing of their movements determine the size, shape, and speed of their turns. The following chart shows how the interplay of balance, rotary, edging, and pressure control skills maintain, decrease, or increase speed of travel.

Factors	Decrease Speed	Maintain or Increase Speed
1. Turn Shape and Turn Completion	a. sharper turn, shorter radius b. arc interrupted by skidding c. more completion	a. shallower turn arc b. carved arc (minimal skidding) c. less completion
2. Edging	a. skidded turn b. more edge than necessary c. hard edge at end of turn d. staying on edge too long	a. clean, carved turn b. minimal edge angle c. releasing the edge at end of turn
3. Weight Distribution	a. weight too far forward, tails skid b. weight too far back, tips skid	a. upper body gets ahead of skis, pulling lower body (shallower arc, less edging as lower body tries to catch up) b. weight back causes skis to go straight, less turn completion

Speed Play chart

CHAPTER 2
GIANT SLALOM

CHAPTER 2 GIANT SLALOM

TECHNIQUE

The turns described in Chapter 1, *Turn Technique*, are Giant Slalom turns. They are dynamic, medium radius, parallel turns. The skills learned in these turns provide the basis for all other parallel turns.

"In my training, Giant Slalom is emphasized. I feel this event requires the most balance, and the truly great champions are Giant Slalom racers. I've had my best results in Downhill because I've always known how to let my skis run. But now I mostly train Giant Slalom and Super-G."
 –Tommy Moe, Olympic Gold and Silver medalist

Dynamic, medium radius, parallel turns

SKILL DEVELOPMENT

Carved Wedge Turns

Wedge turns provide the basis for the skill development of all turns. They are the best test of a skier's ability to blend rotary, edging and pressure control skills in a balanced body position. The difficulties found at the skier's present level will usually be magnified in slow wedge turns since short-comings become obvious while skiing at slow speeds. The coach should use wedge turns to assess a skier's ability to carve and to discover deficiencies that interfere with further learning.

Have the skier perform a series of wedge turns, first on gentle terrain and progressing to steeper pitches. Look for the characteristics, described in Chapter 1, under *Turn Description* which are representative of all efficient and accurate turns both in and out of a race course.

Whenever skiers are on gentle terrain, they should practice wedge turns, focusing on any aspect of technical skiing that needs refinement.

Carved Wedge Turns

Upper Body Position

Excessive upper body movements or actions that compensate for weak lower body skills become more apparent with this exercise. The placement of the skier's poles make hip angulation and a countered position easy to recognize.

Have skiers loop one ski pole strap over the basket of the other pole. Then, have them place the ski poles around the hips and connect the other side. They should make sure the poles are level, before skiing a series of wedge turns. Ideally, the poles should remain parallel to the snow surface. Have skiers notice if the poles tip or turn, indicating:
  a. leaning the upper body into the turn—poles on hips tip instead of staying level
  b. rotating the upper body—poles on hips start the turn before the skis turn
  c. leaning and rotating—poles on hips tip and turn

After a problem has been detected, use this exercise as a visual tool while developing correct movement patterns. Any corrections that are made in the wedge position should be applied to parallel skiing.

Upper Body Position

Wedge/Parallel

This exercise shows the relationship between wedge turns and parallel skiing. The leader turns in a wedge position while the follower skis in a parallel position. The outside ski of the follower is placed in the track of the leader's outside ski.

The follower (parallel skier) can observe the smooth arc of the turn, the action of the outside ski, and the body angles that are developed by the leader (wedge skier). The follower is forced to ski slowly, and therefore can concentrate on feeling the action of the outside ski and developing better body awareness.

Wedge turns and Parallel skiing

Partner Wedge with Slalom Poles

This wedge exercise provides an excellent way to restrain a skier from leaning or rotating into a turn with the upper body.

Have two skiers perform this exercise together, using two Slalom poles. The better technically skilled skier should follow to help position the leader. Without ski poles, the leader holds an end of each Slalom pole while the follower holds the other ends. Have both skiers keep their arms and hands in front of their bodies. Skiers synchronize wedge turns. The Slalom poles make it difficult for either skier to lean inward, and obvious when it does happen. The follower can pull slightly back on the outside pole to encourage a countered position as the leader starts into the turn and continues through the turn.

Body position exercise with partner

Javelin Turns

This exercise emphasizes a countered position with hip angulation. In a javelin, the skier balances on the outside ski of the turn with the inside ski lifted across the front of the outside ski. The placement of the inside ski makes it very difficult to rotate the outside hip through the turn.

Javelin turns can also be used to determine fore/aft balance on the ski. Lifting the tip of the crossed ski higher than the tail usually indicates that the skier's weight is too far in back of the balancing point. When the tail is lifted and the tip is low, the skier's weight may be too far forward.

Alternate, and repeat the following exercises to relate the hip and upper body position of javelin turns to parallel turns:
  a. six linked javelin turns, followed by
  b. six turns lifting the inside ski parallel, followed by
  c. six parallel turns placing the inside ski lightly on the snow

Javelin Turns

Slow Speed Turns

On gentle terrain, at a slow speed, have skiers ski as cleanly as possible through the arc of each turn, maximizing the speed for the situation. Or, in simpler terms, have them ski fast through slow turns! Concentrate on making the skis travel forward through the arc of the turn, with the tails of the skis following the line of the tips. Continue this theme for higher speed turns.

In these turns, use only subtle fore/aft movements to adjust weight forward to start the turn, at the balance point through the turn, and slightly back for the completion of the turn.

Different Turn Shapes

Vary the intensity, duration, and timing of movements to practice "C", "comma", and "J" shaped turns, as described in Chapter 1, under *Turn Description*.

Pole Plant

An effective pole plant is important for purposes of timing, maintaining balance and directing the upper body into an upcoming turn. World Cup racers do not pole plant in every Giant Slalom turn, yet they do plant their poles when necessary, and while free-skiing. Young skiers should plant their poles in Giant Slalom to learn and refine this skill.

Pole Plant

One of the most common problems related to ski pole action is dropping the position of the inside hand after planting the pole. This usually causes the skier to lean toward the inside of the turn and lose the edge hold on the outside ski. For pole usage exercises, and a list of common problems, refer to *Technical Skills for Alpine Skiing*.

GATE DRILLS

Cross-Pole Drill

This exercise addresses the common technical mistake of leaning into the turn. It first exaggerates, and then encourages the proper angle at the hip.

Cross-Pole Drill

Set a rhythmic course of crossed Slalom poles on gentle terrain to be skied in a wedge. Exaggerate tipping the upper body to the outside of the turn as the crossed pole (a1), represents. The wedge position creates the lower body lean indicated by the other pole (a2).

Reset pole (a1) to an upright position (b) to represent the vertical position of the upper body in relation to the lower body in actual skiing. Set a rhythmic course in this way on moderate to steep terrain to be skied in a parallel position. Have skiers transfer to this course the concept and feeling of hip angulation developed in the wedge exercises. As a variation during wedge turns, have skiers hold ski poles horizontally across the body. Be aware if the poles tip inward, indicating the error of leaning into the turn.

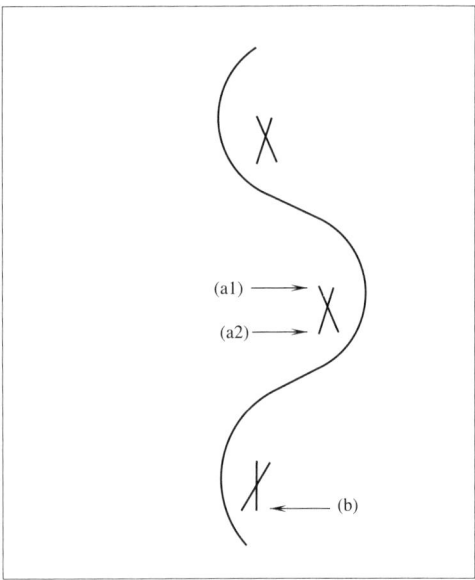
(a1) Exaggerated upper body position (a2) Lower body lean
(b) Vertical upper body position

Creating Courses

Use this exercise to explain how the placement of Slalom poles affects the *racing line* (line through the course).

Set a rhythmic, flowing course of at least ten gates as the basis for this drill (a). Create different rhythms by resetting to vary the course in the following ways. Have skiers run each course three or more times.
  a. Move either the red or the blue poles across the hill in one meter increments. A rounder, tighter course results (b).
  b. Increase the gate distance down the hill in one meter increments. A less "turny", faster course results (c).

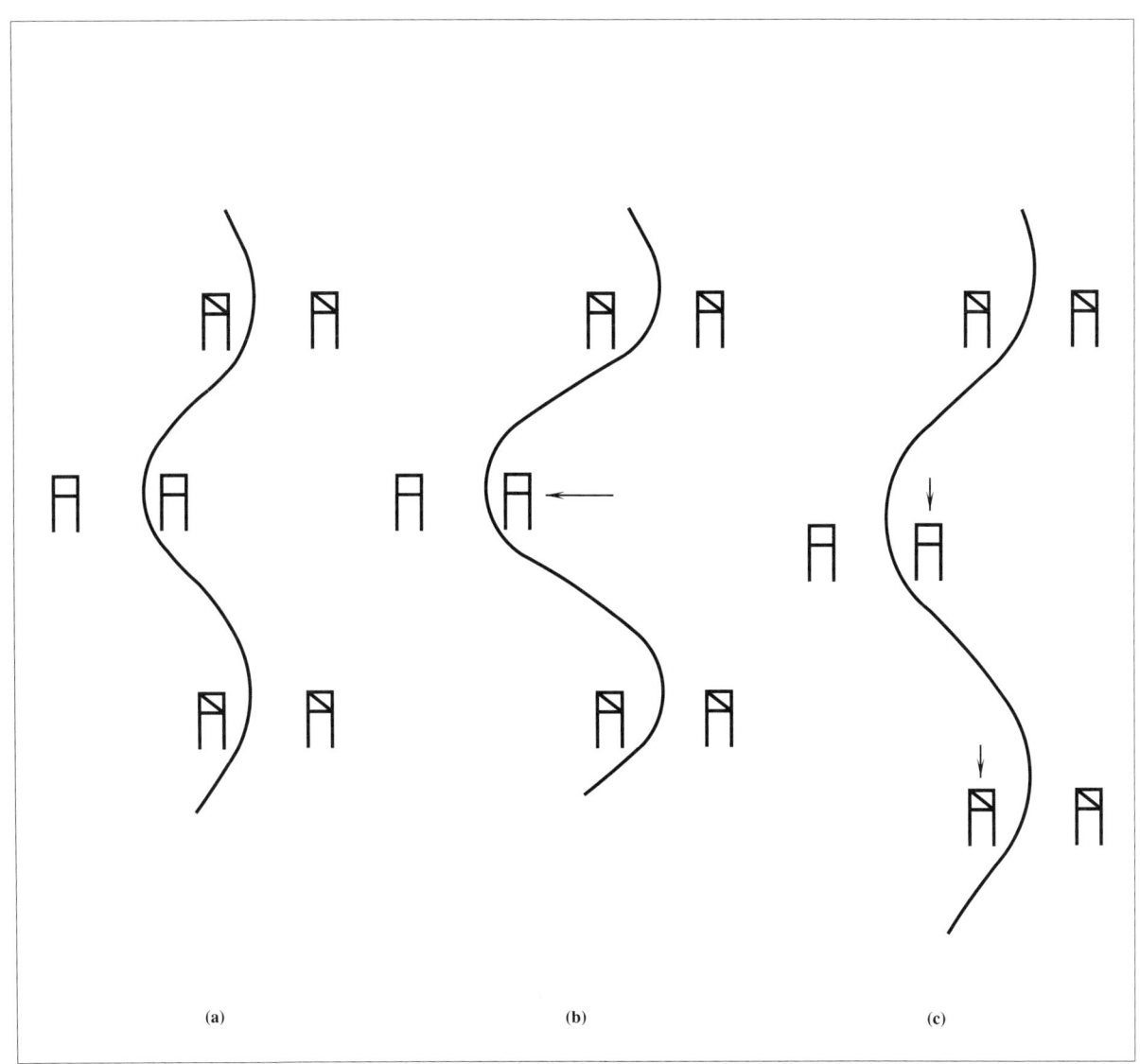

(a) Rhythmic and flowing, (b) Tighter and slower, (c) Faster course

Intermittent Gate Series

This tactical drill requires skiers to rely on visual input in order to make judgments involving the speed, size, and shape of turns. Set rhythmic courses consisting of four to six gates at intervals down a long run. Vary the turn radius for each course. Skiers non-stop the run moving smoothly from the gates into free-skiing and back into the gates. Have skiers make turns of a designated radius between each series of gates. Or, looking ahead, match the turn radius to the line dictated by each upcoming gate series.

One Ski Pole

This experience is important to give racers confidence if they lose a pole at the start, or on the course.

Have skiers run a course with just one, and then just the other ski pole.

No Ski Poles

This technical exercise encourages skiers to maintain a balanced stance.

Have skiers run a practice course without ski poles. Encourage them to stay close to the balance point of the foot so as not to lose balance forward or backward, and to be in position to start each turn. To maintain balance, it is also important for skiers to keep upper body and arm movements quiet.

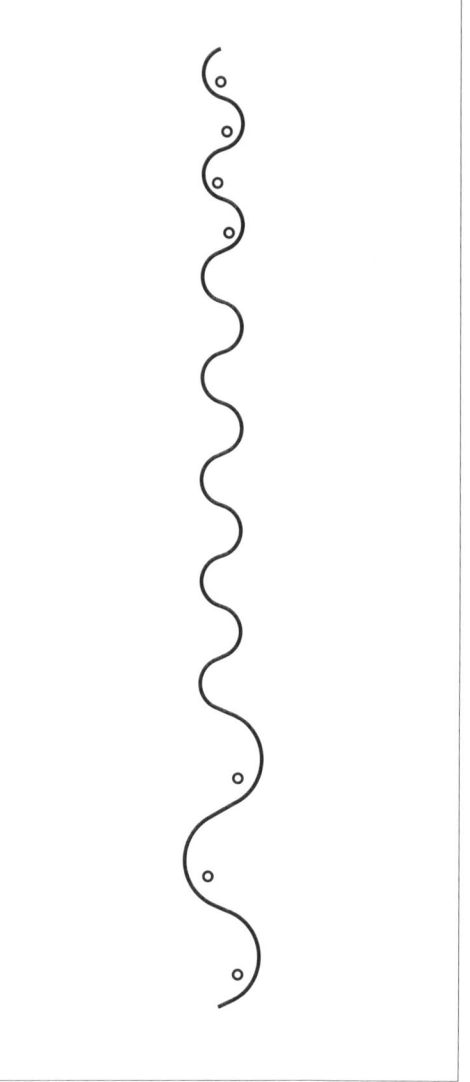

Example of Intermittent Gate Series layout

Intermittent Gate Series

COURSE DESCRIPTION

Regulations and dimensions in this section are derived from the International Ski Federation (FIS) rule book, *The International Ski Competition Rules*. The origin (article number) of each quote is noted in parenthesis.

Open, Closed, Oblique Gate Dimensions

A Giant Slalom course consists of open, closed, and oblique gates. *Open gates* are set horizontally, *closed gates* are set vertically, and *oblique gates* are set diagonally on a hill. Each gate includes four poles and two panels, as drawn. This diagram shows gate dimensions. The distance between poles within a gate is four to eight meters. "The distance between the nearest poles of two successive gates must not be less than ten meters." (901)

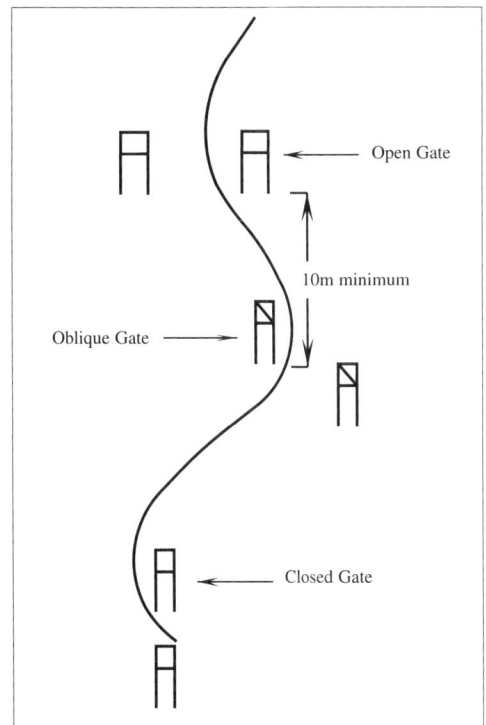

Open, Closed, Oblique Gates

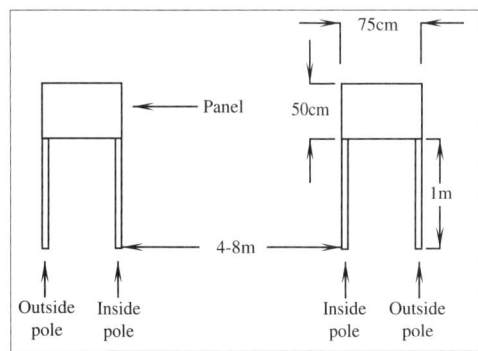

Open Gate Dimensions

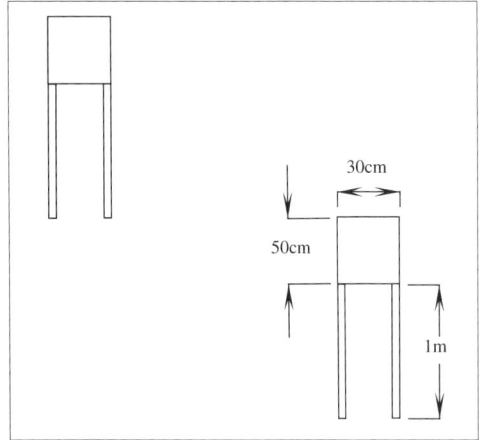

Oblique Gate Dimensions (same for Closed Gates)

Delay Combination

A *delay combination* consists of an open gate, a closed or oblique gate (the delay gate) and another open gate (see Course Diagram). The purpose of the delay is to change the rhythm of the course, or to move the course to a different fall line. Delays are sometimes set to avoid an obstacle or to change to preferred terrain, for example, to move to terrain less rutted from previous courses, or to avoid thin snow cover.

Course Diagram

The corresponding diagram shows a representation of a portion of a course. The path drawn through the course depicts the line of the racer. He/she must cross the *gate line* at every gate. This is the imaginary line between the inside pole of the two panels in a Giant Slalom gate.

Giant Slalom Worksheet

Create worksheets by drawing the gates for Giant Slalom courses. Instruct racers to color gate panels red or blue, label the gates, and draw the skier's line through the course. Blue gate panels have a white diagonal stripe, or other distinctive marks, to make them more visible.

Course Drawing

Have racers create their own courses on paper using the worksheet as an example. This small scale representation of the course should be drawn to show relative distances between gates as well as gate placement. Have the racers label each gate by name and note terrain features. As they learn more about tactics (the skier's line through a course), have them draw the rise line and exit angle (described under *Tactics,* below) for each gate. Then have them draw the racing line through the course. This exercise will test their knowledge and indicate to the coach if there is a lack of understanding.

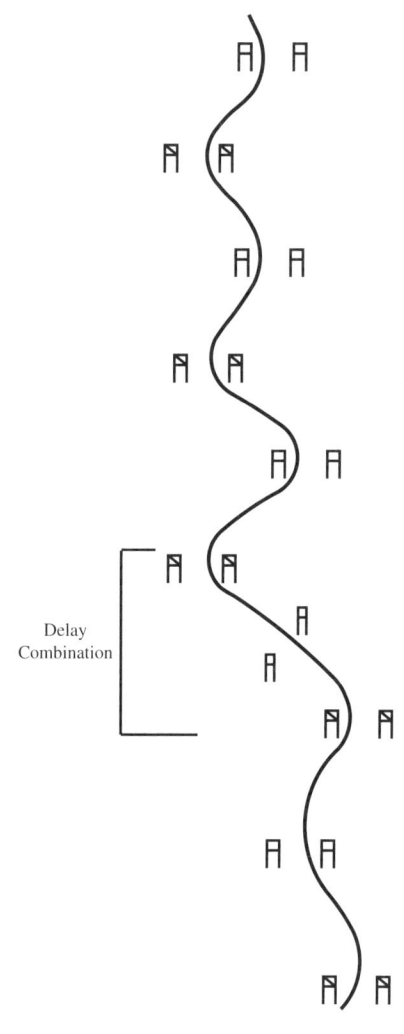

Course Diagram including a Delay Combination

Paper Cup Course

Use red and blue plastic cups to create a miniature Giant Slalom course indoors or on the snow. See *Paper Cup Slalom* for a detailed description in Chapter 3.

Racer Set

When experienced racers understand tactics, let them set and run their own course. This experience will help them learn how courses are set, and therefore, how they should be skied. The coach should emphasize the importance of being able to associate gate placement in relation to terrain and speed.

Paper Cup Course

GIANT SLALOM TACTICS

Tactics refers to the skier's line through a course, also called the *racing line*.

Rise Line

The *rise line* is an imagined line that extends above the turning pole of each gate. For all gates (open, closed, and oblique), turns should be started on the rise line. The specific location along the rise line is at the point that will allow the skier to execute a smooth turn in which the direction change is finished as he/she goes by the pole (a). Turns that are started too low on the rise line will result in a low line below the gate (b). If too sharp a turn is attempted, the skier will usually skid to a lower line, as well. Turns that are started too high above the gate will require a rounder and larger radius than is necessary. Or if a tighter radius is attempted, the completion of the turn will aim into the gate (c). As a result, the skier will have to come out of the turn and then reestablish the line. This adjustment results in skidding. Starting a turn too early, before the rise line, will also aim the skier into the gate (d). He/she will have to release the edge and skid, moving sideways to be clear of the pole. Starting the turn late, after the rise line, will result in a wider turn than may be necessary (e). Any of these adjustments will be slow compared to skiing the optimum line (f).

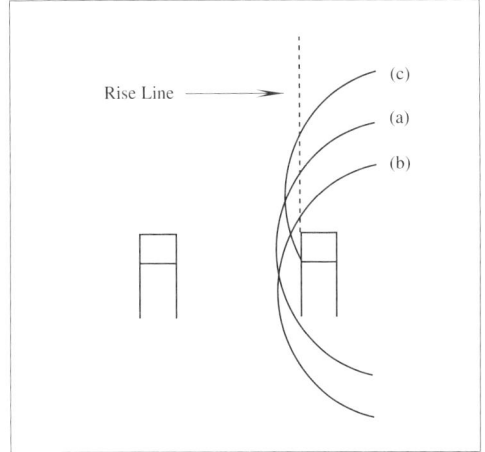

(a) Optimum line, (b) Low line, (c) Aim into the gate

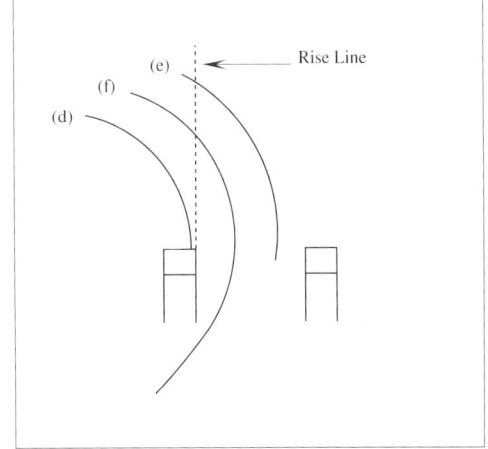

(d) Aim into the gate, (e) Wide turn, (f) Optimum line

Rise Line (Continued)

Gates placed across the hill dictate a "turny" course. For sharper turns, the turn should be initiated higher on the rise line as illustrated in gate (b) in order to complete the turn by the gate. Gates set closer to the fall line require less of a turn. The skier should start these turns lower on the rise line as illustrated in gate (d).

An oblique gate should be approached in the same way as an open gate. The difference is that the visual absence of an outside pole, located on a horizontal plane, makes it difficult to gauge the set of the course.

Exit Angle

Exit angle refers to the direction the skis aim when the racer goes by the turning pole. At this point, the turn should be completed with the skis redirected in preparation for the upcoming turn. In a "turny" section of a course, the skis will be at a greater angle to the fall line than in a relatively straight section. The rounder the turns, the farther across the hill the skis should point as illustrated in gate (a) in order to be set up for the next gate. For gates set closer to the fall line, the skis should point straighter down the hill as shown in gate (c).

For rhythm changes, start to adjust the line one or two gates in advance to make a smooth transition. For example, use a rounder line for an upcoming "turny" section; straighter line approaching fall line turns.

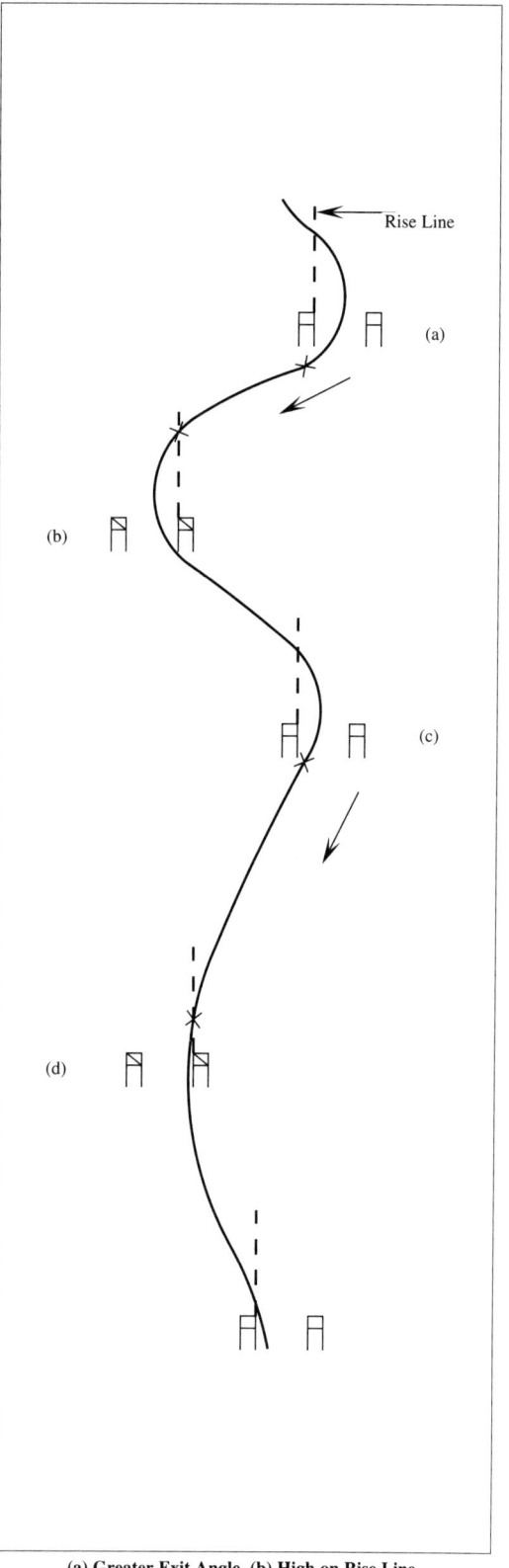

(a) Greater Exit Angle, (b) High on Rise Line,
(c) Less Exit Angle, (d) Lower on Rise Line

Closer Line

An experienced racer who can ski a closer (tighter) line to a gate can start the turn a little lower on the rise line (a) than a less capable racer (b). At the completion of the turn, the skis of the more experienced racer point straighter down the hill in comparison to the exit angle of the less competent skier. The speed of travel and the skier's ability to make a precise turn are factors to consider in determining the best line.

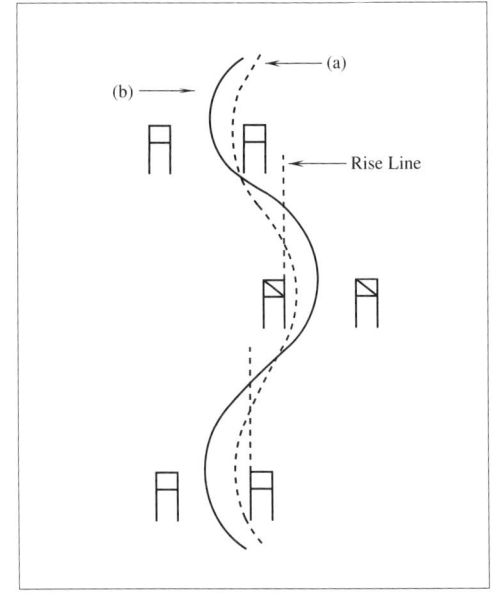

(a) Closer line, (b) Wider line

Delay the Turn

In large changes of direction, it may be necessary to delay the turn—start the turn *after* crossing the rise line (a) in order to complete the turn at the gate. This tactic is also known as "come-from-behind" since the turn is started from behind the turning pole. In relation to turning around this pole, most of the turn occurs above the gate. This is accomplished by redirecting the skis early in the turn to cut through the end of the turn. This requires a high edge angle and pressure very early in the turn.

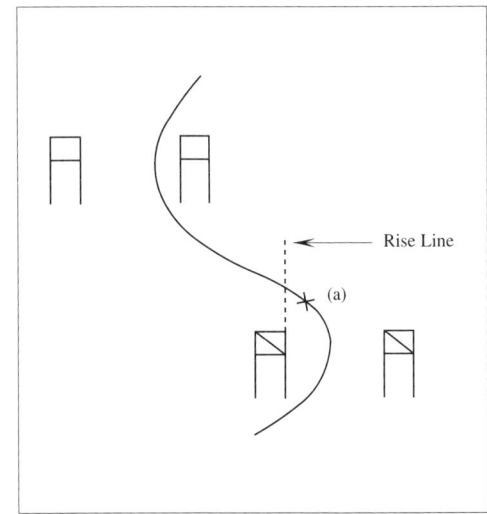

(a) Turn starts after the Rise Line

Delay the Turn

Transition Between Turns

The transition between turns can be skied in different ways. The fastest approach for any given situation is dictated by the demands of the course. To ski through the transition, one of the following methods, or a combination of these, can be used. At first, work on these variations out of the gates.
 a. Stay on the outside, edged ski to continue turning.
 b. Transfer weight to the uphill ski to glide across the hill. Weight taken off the turning and edged outside ski is placed on a non-turning and flatter ski. This will allow the skier to carry more speed across the hill (pictured).
 c. Glide on two skis to reduce the degree of edge and pressure on the outside ski. As a result, the skis will not turn as much, if at all. The outside ski will be comparatively flatter on the snow and, therefore, travel faster.

Weight transfer to the uphill ski

Helper Poles/Markers

Helper poles, or other markers, provide visual points of reference for teaching tactics. Surveyor flags, *SAF T STIKS*, or marking the snow with dye made from food coloring provide safe markers that will not injure the skier upon contact.

It is easier to position markers if the coach (or a tactically skilled racer) first skis the proper line, and then uses the tracks as reference for the placement of the markers.

Set a marker on each rise line to remind racers to wait until that point to start the turn. The marker can also dictate the height above the gate at which the turn should be started. Position the marker so that racers pass just above it.

(a) Proper line

Set a marker below each gate that is positioned just beneath the skier's line. The racers also ski above this marker. Skiing into the marker will be avoided when technically correct form on the proper line is achieved (a).

Helper Poles/Markers (Continued)

This series of photographs (b) reveals the consequence of starting the turn too early, that is, before the rise line.

(b) Turn started too early (photo sequence)

Helper Poles/Markers (Continued)

After many runs, slip and inspect the course with the racers to increase their understanding. At this time, remove the rise line markers. Have racers ski the course while continuing to concentrate on their line. Finally, remove the lower markers while maintaining the proper line (c).

Set a new course for the racers to inspect and run, focusing on what they have learned from the helper poles/markers exercise.

Remove markers

Delay Combination

Racers should start a delay combination high on the rise line of the first open gate in order to establish the direction change necessary to continue through the closed/oblique gate. The greater length of this turn often makes it difficult to wait for the rise line of the second open gate. The optimum position above this gate is determined by the placement of gates following the delay.

For large changes of direction, it may be necessary to start the turn after crossing the rise line of one or both open gates in a delay combination.

The placement of the upper pole in the closed/oblique gate may not interfere with the line between open gates, or on the other hand, it can dictate the line. In the latter case, as diagrammed, the upper pole of the delay gate becomes the turning pole (b). As a result, the racer may need to ski wide on the first open gate (a) in order to be on line for the delay gate.

The panels on the delay gate are distinguishable because they are narrower than open gate panels.

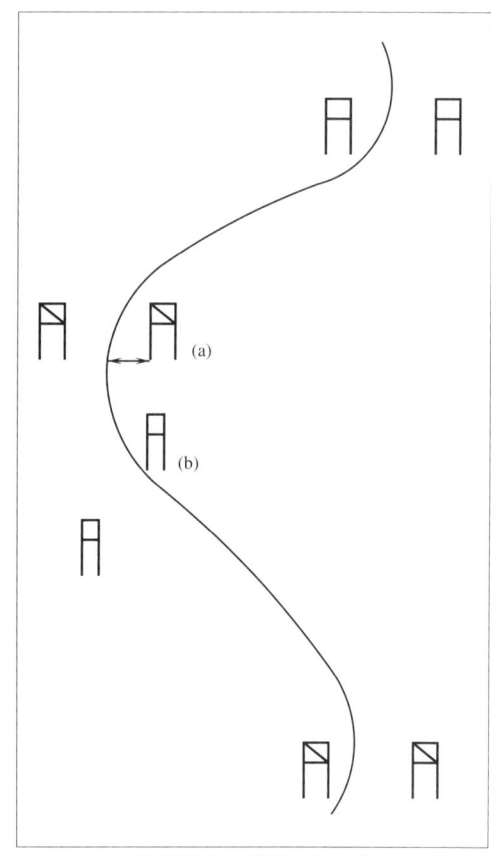

(a) Wide line, (b) Turning pole

Delay Combination (Continued)

These photographs show a racer skiing through a delay combination.

Delay Combination (photo sequence)

Look Ahead

This exercise helps skiers learn to look farther ahead while skiing, giving them more time to prepare for terrain changes or to choose a line through a race course.

On a chair lift, have skiers look at the chair in front of theirs. Then, while still viewing that chair, focus on the one beyond. With practice, skiers will be able to view simultaneously the chair in front, the one beyond, and the one beyond that.

Read Terrain

This exercise develops visual awareness which is necessary for adapting to terrain in or out of a race course.

Have skiers describe terrain immediately after they ski a trail. They should be able to identify steepness, transitions, sidehills, rolls, and bumps. Does the trail wind down the mountain, turning to the left or right?

Mind Set

This exercise develops perceptual skills by combining elements of speed and distance in relation to terrain.

Have skiers imagine they will set a course on selected terrain. They will have to vary the placement of gates to correspond to this terrain. Where on the hill will they set the poles to dictate rounded turns to control speed? Where will they set the poles closer to the fall line to let the skis run? How will they set the poles to bring the course across the hill to move to different terrain?

Course Inspection

All courses, even drill courses, should be inspected prior to skiing them. Racers must sideslip and not ski the course during inspection.

Have racers stop on the rise line (a) during course inspection to study the optimum racing line in relation to gate placement. Have them look up the hill at the previous gate and down toward the upcoming gates. Then, have them find the point at which they feel their skis should cross the rise line. In this way, racers can gain a general sense of how high they will need to be above the gate in order to make a smooth turn, finishing at the gate. Then, have the racers slip below the Slalom pole to stand at the exit angle position (b). Have them find the angle at which their skis should be positioned in order to set up for the next gate. As a guide, point the skis toward the outside pole of the upcoming gate for very round turns. For a less "turny" gate, point the skis toward the middle of the next gate. Point the skis toward the inside third of the upcoming gate for fall line turns.

Inexperienced racers should be led through course inspection and taught what to look for when they inspect on their own. Make note of general terrain and specific terrain changes, for example, steep, flat or sidehill slopes, trail direction changes, rolls, knolls, etc. Also, bring attention to rhythm sections and rhythm changes. Have racers visualize the course after course inspection. Have them take turns verbalizing perceptions. This will help racers be aware of different aspects, such as terrain, course set, and self-talk, e.g.: "set up...now", "round, round, quick!" When they have gained confidence in these skills, give a verbal start command for them to leave the start and race the course in their minds. The amount of time it takes to "ski" the visualized course should be similar to their actual skiing time.

(a) Rise Line

(b) Exit Angle

CHAPTER 3
SLALOM

CHAPTER 3 SLALOM

TECHNIQUE

The information contained in Chapter 1, *Turn Technique*, provides the basis for all Slalom turns. Slalom turns are short radius, dynamic, parallel turns. Compared to longer radius turns, the rhythm of turns and pace of movements is quicker. The following technical information is specific to Slalom turns.

Upper Body Position

In general, the skier's upper body faces down the hill throughout the turn. There is not time for the upper body to follow the direction of the skis. Nor is there time for excessive arm movements to occur or hinder balance.

Ski Pole Action

The pole plant is used for blocking upper body rotation as well as for timing. Wrist movement is used primarily to swing the pole tip forward. In turns with a deliberate edge set, the pole plant and edge set occur at the same time. In gliding turns, the pole touch occurs a moment later, with the extension at the initiation of the next turn.

Hand Position

When athletes have reached an all-around skill level that allows them to clear Slalom poles out of the way, they can practice holding their hands in a higher position for this purpose. Slalom poles will flex more easily and move away when contacted at a higher point. Hands should be positioned with the thumb of each hand turned slightly inward, so that the ski pole points slightly outward instead of straight down. From this position, the Slalom pole is knocked away by contact with the ski pole shaft. Contact with the ski pole should be made just below the grip. Immediately afterward, the appropriate ski pole should be planted for the next turn.

Less technically skilled skiers should not use the higher hand position. It has the tendency to move the skier's weight back, which would oppose good balance and movement down the hill.

Dynamic, short radius, parallel turns

Clearing Flex Poles

Now that plastic "flex" poles are used, i.e., poles that bend at the snow surface, racers can move the pole out of the way for a more direct line down the course. The *clearing* action should not upset the position of the skier's upper body, nor the quality of the turn. There are different ways to ski past a Slalom pole:

   a. Skiing around the Slalom pole is always the first step before learning to move "through" poles. It is also the method to use with the more rigid bamboo poles, and to negotiate round turns on very steep terrain. These turns require strong countered and angulated positions in which the outside arm is directed down the hill, and not in position to clear the pole.

   The racer skis a round line, lightly brushing or not touching the pole.

   b. The *inside hand clear* method is used in flushes. It can also be used for round turns on steep terrain as described above. The difference is that the skier's line is closer to the gate.

   The Slalom pole is cleared out of the way by placement of the inside hand (hand closest to the pole). The forearm crosses slightly in front of the body, without affecting the upper body position, to come into contact with the Slalom pole. Then, both hands remain relatively quiet, or move slightly forward as the racer's momentum down the hill knocks the pole out of the way.

Skiing around the pole

Inside hand clear (Flush)

Inside hand clear (Delay)

c. The *outside hand clear* is the most common method of clearing since it allows racers to ski very close to the Slalom poles for the fastest line possible. This line places the racer's upper body to the inside of the Slalom pole. Therefore, with little movement, the outside hand is in position to clear the pole. This action is also known as the "cross block".

The Slalom pole is cleared out of the way by the placement of the outside hand. The outside hand crosses in front of the body without affecting the upper body position. Hands remain relatively quiet, or move slightly forward, as the skier's momentum down the hill knocks the pole out of the way. This technique requires special attention because rotation and/or leaning problems can be created by crossing the outside hand past the center of the body. These problems often occur when the racer's line is too far from the poles for clearing with the outside hand to be effective.

Outside hand clear

d. Racers *shin* Slalom poles to clear them out of the way by contact with the shins. Shinning is not as effective as hand clearing. Since the shaft is hit lower to the base of the flex pole, there is less leverage, and therefore, it requires more force to clear the pole in this way. Shinning may be necessary when the racer's hands are already being used to regain balance. Since it requires more body mass and force to clear poles in this manner, it is not an appropriate method for young skiers.

SKILL DEVELOPMENT

Turn Versatility

It is necessary to be a technically skilled skier in order to become an accomplished racer. Skiers should practice consistent and varying size Slalom turns out of the gates to be versatile and able to adapt to the different demands of race courses. Different technical elements of short radius turns can provide focus for a run, such as, balancing on the outside ski, planting poles, and facing the upper body down the hill.

a. Have skiers practice smooth, round, short radius turns over a long distance, maintaining *consistent* turn size, speed and rhythm. Then the intensity of the exercise can be changed to achieve "snappy" turns by aggressively steering and increasing the edge angle of the ski.

Have skiers practice consistent turns on gentle terrain, progressing to a very steep slope.

b. Have skiers *vary* the shape, size, and rhythm of short radius turns without abrupt changes in speed. He/she should direct upper body movement down the hill to flow smoothly through transitions between turns.

Have skiers practice first on smooth terrain, progressing to small bumps and inconsistent terrain. This exercise requires skiers to look ahead and adapt to the demands presented by varying terrain.

Lead/Follow Medley

This game promotes versatility, quick responses, and skill improvement.

The follower stays in the leader's tracks as he/she varies the radius of turns. The leader includes an assortment of exercises in his/her descent. The follower attempts to perform the exercises when in the same turn at which the exercise was performed by the leader. Examples of exercises to include in the medley are:
    a. lift the inside ski off the snow
    b. lift the outside ski off the snow
    c. plant just the right or left ski poles
    d. do not plant poles
    e. jump at the initiation of each turn
    f. 360° turn

Arms Crossed

This exercise is used to develop strong lower body skills. The skier should ski without poles and with arms crossed (hands touching the shoulders). The cross of the arms should point down the hill to limit unnecessary upper body movement. The skier should make a deliberate weight transfer onto the outside ski followed by a strong turning action of both skis as they are tipped on edge.

Excessive upper body movements become more apparent with this exercise. Look for the following problems:
    a. rotating the upper body into the turn
    b. leaning the upper body into the turn; shoulders tip instead of staying level
    c. leaning and rotating into the turn
    d. bending forward at the waist

After practicing with arms crossed, have skiers hold their

Arms Crossed

hands in front of their bodies, continuing to emphasize lower body action. Next, have them add the ski poles, and finally, add rhythmic pole plants. They should use the wrist to bring the pole tip forward and to discourage nonessential arm movements.

Excessive upper body motion often compensates for a lack of proper leg action. The exercises in Level 4 of *Technical Skills for Alpine Skiing*, will also help to develop correct movement patterns.

Tuck Turns

Tuck turns develop strong rotary movements of the lower body which allow the racer to make quick turns. In the tuck position, the upper body is restricted, forcing the legs to control the skis.

Have the skier start in a high tuck position on gentle terrain. (Description of high and low tuck positions are under *Technique* in Chapter 4.) Hands should be aimed down the hill to direct the upper body. Have skiers turn just a little out of the fall line at first, then progress to greater changes of direction. Weight transfer to the new outside ski of the turn is important for starting each turn. Have skiers progress to a lower tuck position, linking round, short radius turns.

Have skiers alternate tuck turns with Slalom turns, retaining a stable upper body in both cases, as the lower body creates the turn.

Synchronized Shadow

This exercise provides an excellent opportunity for the coach to express the direct relationship between sound technical skiing and racing.

While one person skis a rhythmic Slalom course, the other skier shadows the course, i.e., skis along the side of the course, out of the gates, following the line of the course. The shadow skier stays synchronized with the gate skier. After both skiers have experienced the shadow role, set a new course as diagrammed. Each skier flows into and out of short courses.

Tuck Turns

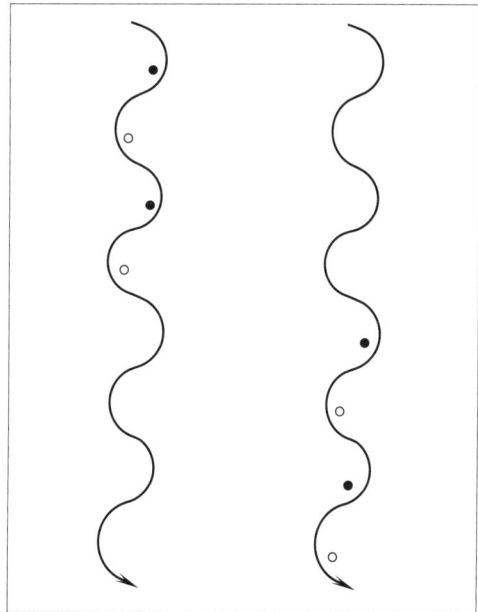
Synchronized Shadow layout

Synchronized Shadow

Synchronized Speed Play

Racers must be versatile skiers in order to adjust to any situation and maximize every opportunity to go faster. This exercise uses the interplay of rotary, edging, and pressure control skills to affect the speed of travel down a hill.

One person skis consistent, rhythmic, short radius turns. *Staying synchronized*, another skier starts alongside (a), then falls back (b–c), and catches up (d) in relation to the consistent skier. Throughout the series of turns, both skiers start and end each turn at the same moment. It is helpful for the variable speed skier to continue the turn rhythm by using the consistent skier's pole plant as a timing cue.

The chart under *Speed Play* in Chapter 1, describes different ways to decrease, increase and maintain speed.

(a) Start position

(b) Skier falls back

(c) Skier falls farther back

(d) Skier catches up

Synchronized Circle

This exercise is a variation of *Synchronized Speed Play*. It also uses the interplay of skills to control the speed of descent.

One skier skis consistent, rhythmic, short radius turns. *Staying* synchronized, another skier leads (a), pulls out to the side (b–c), circles behind (d), and advances to the other side of the consistent skier (e–f).

(a) Start position

(b) Leader poles out

(c) Leader alongside

(d) Leader circles behind

Synchronized Circle (Continued)

(e) Leader advances

(f) Leader advances to other side

Line Pull-out

The *Line Pull-out* is a variation of the *Synchronized Circle* that involves four or more skiers. It provides yet another opportunity for skiers to practice short radius turns.

The skiers start in a vertical line and follow the leader's tracks (not synchronized). The leader skis consistent, rhythmic, short radius turns. After leading for a designated number of turns (six, for example), the leader pulls out to the side of the vertical line and the next-in-line becomes the leader for six turns. This process continues with each skier taking a turn at leading the line. When skiers pull away from the vertical line, they continue to turn, slowing their speed in order for the whole line to pass. Then they join the end of the line as the whole revolving process continues.

Hand Position Exercises

These exercises can be used to teach hand position for clearing Slalom poles:

a. Over the period of many free-skiing runs, have skiers raise their hands a few inches at a time until they are almost at shoulder height. Then, have skiers alternate between low and high hand positions during different runs to maintain versatility. In both positions, the skier should start each turn with weight forward of the

Hand position exercise

balance point of the foot.

b. The double pole plant is a good drill to help skiers position both hands up and forward. Both ski poles are planted at the same time. The pole action also helps skiers recover from a low position at the turn completion. It discourages rotation of the shoulders and encourages level shoulders.

After practicing this drill, have skiers return to a single pole plant, maintaining a stable body position with both hands up and forward.

GATE DRILLS

Two Meter Drill

This drill develops the technical elements of a balanced stance, strong lower body rotary skills, and a quiet upper body. It also encourages an efficient pole plant.

Set Slalom poles in the fall line approximately two meters apart (the length of a 200 cm ski) on a moderate to steep slope. Have skiers link hop turns around the poles, landing on edged skis and hopping off edged skis, without skidding. They should wait until their ski boots slide past the pole before hopping. It is important to maintain a balanced body position with the upper body facing down the hill. A solid pole plant supports and stabilizes the hopping action and helps to continue rhythm and movement.

The two meter drill can also be set in a moderate to steep traverse instead of along the fall line.

Foot Placement

Set rhythmic courses using the teaching aids described below to work toward a racing line that is close to the poles. Tactical exercises using these aids will allow racers to develop ski/foot placement before they learn clearing techniques.
    a. *Stubby poles* are flex poles that are about two feet tall and taped or padded at the top.
    b. *SAF T STIKs*, used in this photograph, are lightweight, soft and non-intimidating.
    c. Cones, such as traffic cones
    d. Markers, such as surveyor flags

After racers can consistently shin a practice course set with

Two Meter Drill

Using teaching aids for ski/foot placement

short-length poles, add a couple of full length poles for the purpose of developing clearing skills while maintaining the same line.

Slalom Pole Clearing Exercises

It is important for racers to be well versed with different options of attack through a course. Racers can become versatile by developing a variety of clearing skills in order to meet course demands efficiently and effectively. The following sequence of drills uses a rhythmic course of twelve gates (alternating red and blue poles) to help develop these skills. Repeat the course having racers perform the following tasks:
- a. Ski around all of the poles without touching them.
- b. Clear all of the poles with the inside hand. Repeat with the outside hand.
- c. Clear the first six poles with the inside hand, clear the last six poles with the outside hand.
- d. Clear the first six poles with the outside hand, ski around the last six poles.
- e. Clear only the blue poles with the inside hand. Ski around the red poles. Then, clear only the red poles with the inside hand. Ski around the blue poles.
- f. Clear only the blue poles with the outside hand. Ski around the red poles. Then, clear only the red poles with the outside hand. Ski around the blue poles.

Short Courses

Short courses of approximately ten to twelve gates can help to develop aggressive skiing. They are less intimidating and tiring than long courses, therefore allowing the racer to focus on specific technical and tactical elements. Examples are balance on the outside ski, or, wait for the rise line.

Rhythmic and flowing course

The following short courses can be timed with skiers trying to better their results each run through the course. Diagrams follow on the next page.
- a. Courses that are rhythmic and flowing (a).
- b. Overly round courses in which poles are set farther across the hill (b).
- c. Overly tight courses in which the vertical distance between turning poles is decreased (c).
- d. Courses that contain one rhythm change (d).
- e. Hourglass courses in which round turns gradually change to fall line turns, then gradually return to round turns (e).
- f. Hairpin, turn, hairpin, turn... (f)

Overly round course

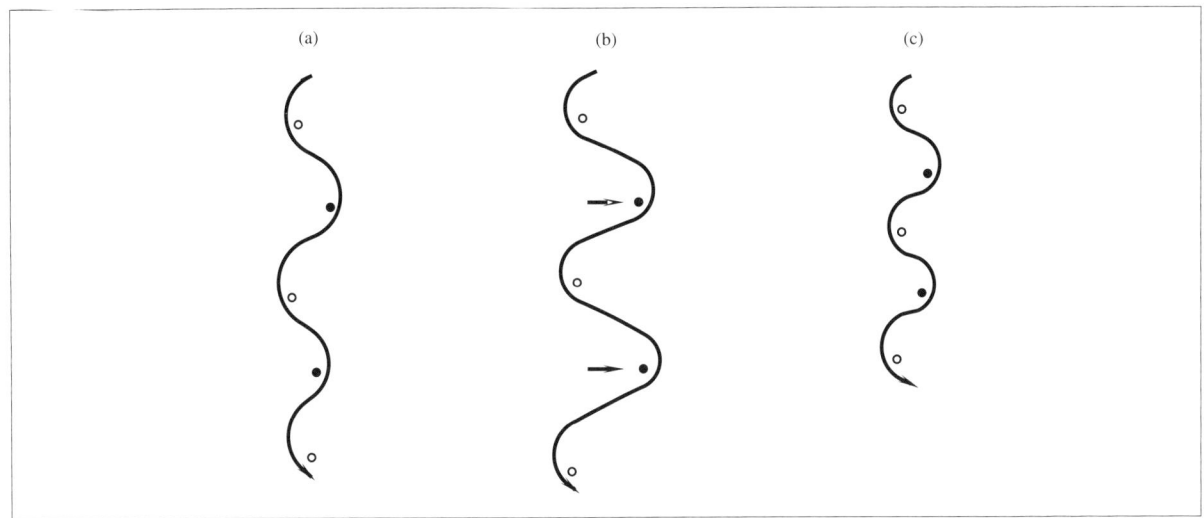

(a) Rhythmic, (b) Overly round, (c) Overly tight

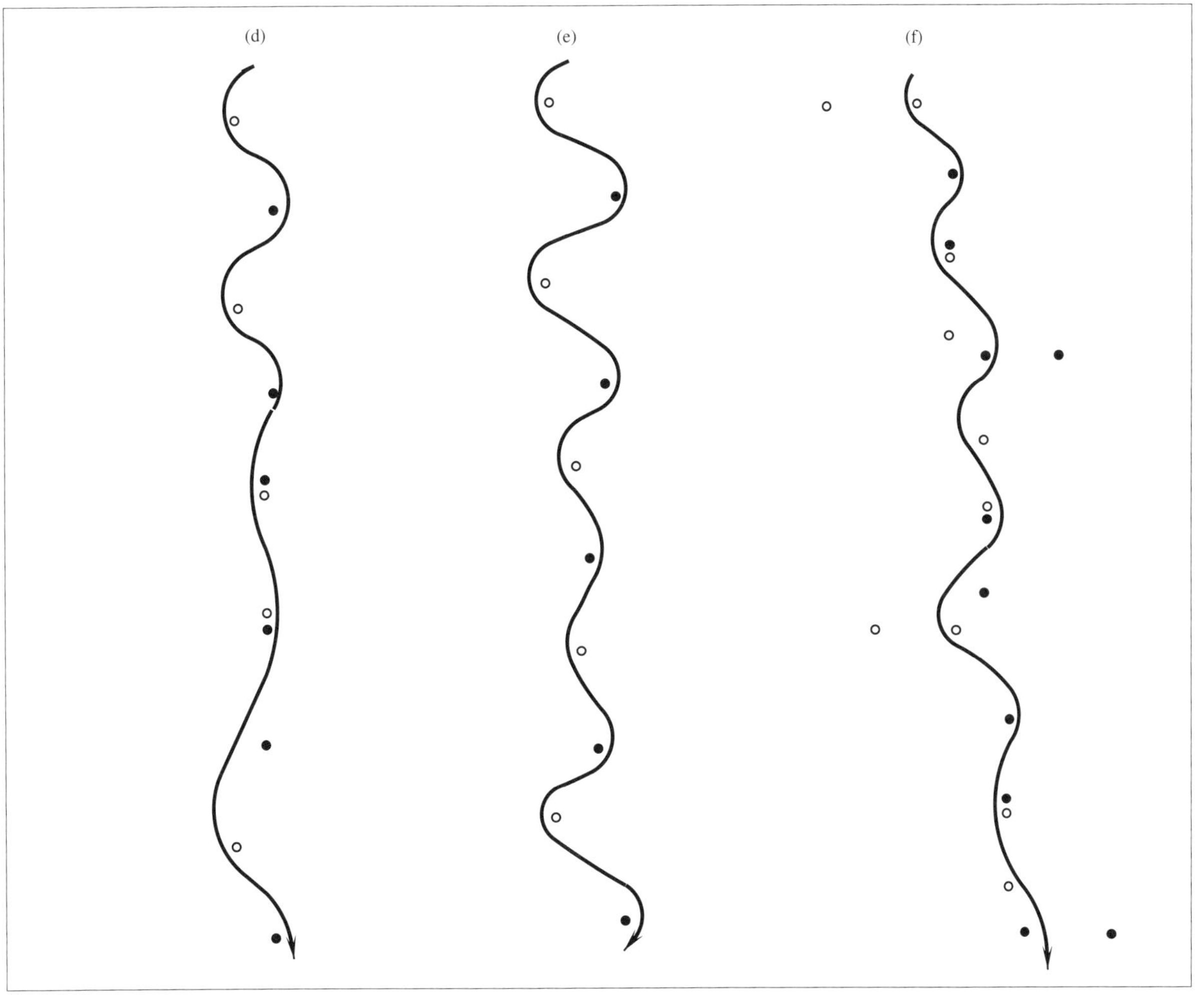

(d) One rhythum change, (e) Hourglass, (f) Hairpin, turn

41

Course Rotation

Set the following drill courses across a slope. Skiers rotate through short courses, of twelve to sixteen turns, skiing one course per run, followed by free-skiing to the next course. This set-up encourages plenty of directed free-skiing time (skiing with technical goals in mind) before and after each drill course. The focus of the drill course can be continued out of the gates. For example, the focus can be on correct hand position, balancing on the outside ski, completing each turn, etc. This format keeps all of the racers moving, seldom waiting for a turn.

If a wide slope is not available, set the courses down a run, leaving adequate room to stop between courses. Still, ski only one course per run.

Use the following course rotations and create others to assist in the skier's development.
  a. Set a corridor of poles two to three ski lengths wide. Within the corridor, skiers perform hop turns, outside ski hop turns (a), turns on one ski (b), turns without ski poles (c), turns with arms crossed, etc. Change the exercise each time through the corridor.
  b. Set a rhythmic course with bamboo or flex poles. Have skiers ski around the poles with minimal contact (d).
  c. Set a rhythmic course with stubby poles, *SAF T STIKs*, cones, or markers (e).
  d. Set a rhythmic course with flex poles to focus on outside hand clearing technique (f).

(a) Outside ski hop turns

(b) Turns on one ski

(c) Turns without ski poles

(d) Ski around poles

(e) Ski around markers

(f) Outside hand clear

COURSE DESCRIPTION

Regulations and dimensions in this section are derived from the International Ski Federation (FIS) rule book, *The International Ski Competition Rules*. The origin (article number) of each reference is noted in parenthesis.

Gate Dimensions

The corresponding diagram labels the elements of a Slalom gate, shows the dimensions, and gives the measurements for the vertical distance between gates (801 and 803). An open gate (horizontal), an oblique gate (diagonal), and closed gates (vertical) are illustrated.

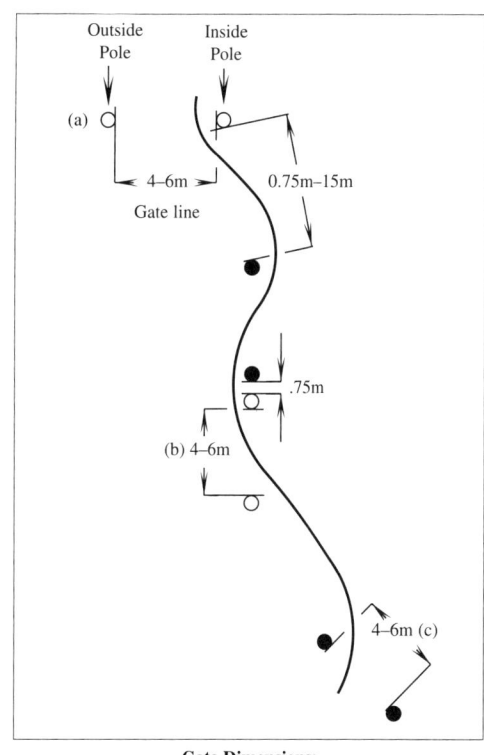

Gate Dimensions:
(a) Open Gate, (b) Closed Gate, (c) Oblique gate

Description of Combinations

Hairpin, flush and delay gate combinations are illustrated in the corresponding diagram. Hairpins and flushes contain only closed gates and therefore, are named, *vertical combinations*. A *hairpin* consists of two closed gates. The racer can either ski over (higher than) the top pole (*over-hairpin*) or below the top pole (*into-hairpin*) of the first closed gate. A flush consists of three or four closed gates. A delay combination consists of an open gate, a closed or oblique gate (the delay gate) and another open gate. It is not considered to be a vertical combination.

A FIS Slalom course must have at least three hairpins (over-hairpins and/or into-hairpins), and no less than one or more than three flushes consisting of three to four gates.

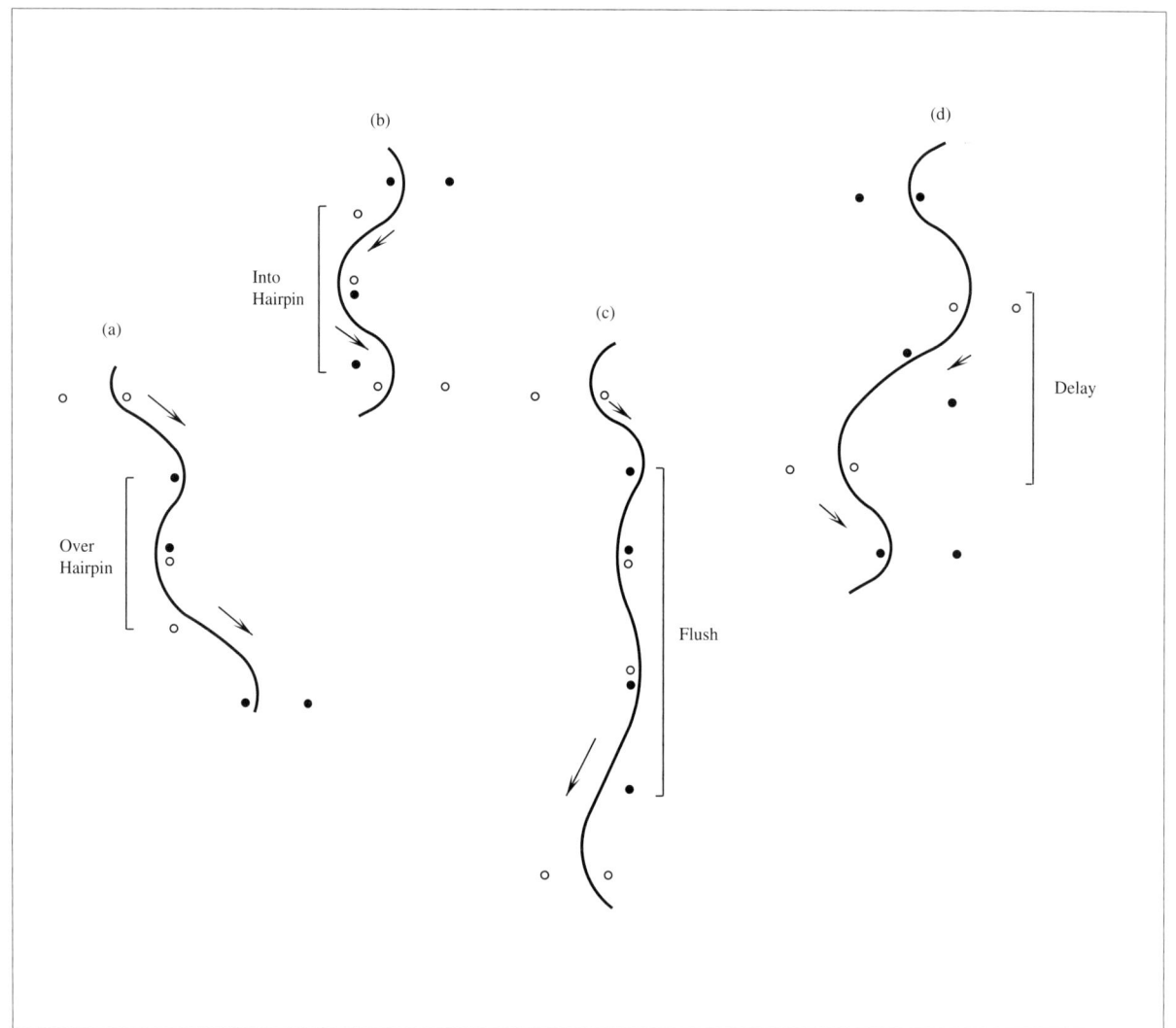

(a) Over-hairpin, (b) Into-hairpin, (c) Flush, (d) Delay

Course Diagram

A Slalom course consists of open, closed, and oblique gates, as well as hairpin, flush and delay gate combinations. The following diagram illustrates gates and some gate combinations. Circles are used to represent poles.

Slalom Worksheet

On paper, draw the gates for a Slalom course. Instruct skiers to color the poles (represented by circles) red and blue, label the gates and gate combinations, and draw the skier's line through the course.

Course Drawing

Have racers draw their own courses. This activity will test knowledge and indicate any lack of understanding. From the drawings, determine on-the-snow courses that will reinforce the corrections made on paper.

When racers can draw a course correctly, assign tasks for subsequent drawings. Some examples are:
    a. The start is at the upper right corner of the paper. Draw the course to finish in the lower left corner.
    b. Include two over-hairpins and one into-hairpin in the course.
    c. Label the paper according to terrain features, such as, steep slope, sidehill, turn in the trail, knoll. Then, use the terrain features to determine the placement of gates.
    d. Draw a course that has many changes in rhythm.

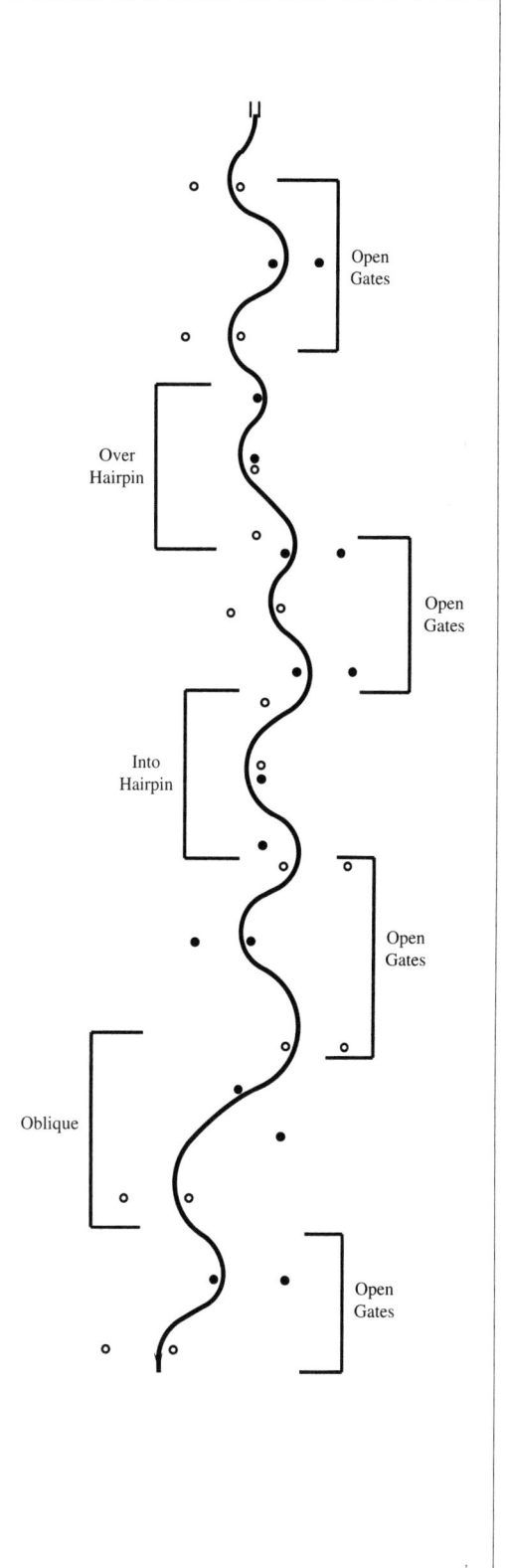

Course Diagram

45

Paper Cup Slalom

Use red and blue plastic cups to create a miniature Slalom course on a floor or on the snow. Use this course to describe gate combinations, gate placement and line. People can walk through the course, identifying gates and conceptualizing line. Set a variety of courses to make different points. The difference between an over and into-hairpin can be illustrated, gate combinations to avoid obstacles (gloves can represent obstacles) can be represented. The influence of imagined changes in trail direction or terrain can be discussed.

Have racers create their own paper cup courses. Invent situations to encourage them to think and solve problems. For example, assume the top of the course is very steep, midway down the course the snow cover is thin, at the bottom section of the course the trail curves to the left.

Racer Set

After racers have experienced setting a Giant Slalom course, have them set portions of Slalom courses. The first experience should center around setting rhythmical, open gates. Next, have racers set open gates exhibiting rhythm changes. Gate combinations could be set in the next course. Have racers ski each portion and discuss with the coach the changes they would make to improve the course. This learning experience will help them better understand how courses are set and, therefore, how they should be skied.

Paper Cup Slalom

SLALOM TACTICS

Rise Line

Rise line is discussed in Chapter 2, under *Giant Slalom Tactics*.

In Slalom, racers start their turns lower on the rise line than in Giant Slalom because the radius of a Slalom turn is much smaller.

Exit Angle

Exit angle is discussed in Chapter 2, under *Giant Slalom Tactics*.

In regard to turn shape, a "comma" turn allows skiers to achieve the desired exit angle at the completion of the turn.

Comma turns are fast since the direction change occurs above the gate, where there is less pressure on the ski. A "J" turn is slow because most of the direction change occurs below the gate, in the second half of the turn. This creates additional pressure where pressure is already at its greatest. As a result, the racer often skids to a low line, below the ideal exit angle.

A "C" turn can be either fast or slow depending on the location of the turn in relation to the gate placement. When the turn is initiated at the appropriate point along the rise line, the racer will be on target and aligned with the exit angle. Turn shapes are described in greater detail and drawn in Chapter 1, under *Turn Shapes*.

Hairpin

In an *over-hairpin*, the racer skis above the top pole of the first closed gate. An over-hairpin designates a quick change in the rhythm of a course. Racers enter and then exit over-hairpins traveling in the same direction. Usually, course setters will set the upper pole of the first closed gate in rhythm with the preceding open gates, or they will set this pole farther across the hill to control speed before entering fall line turns (closed gates). Course setters tend to set for a straighter path coming out of a combination by allowing more vertical distance. This compensates for the speed gained from skiing down the fall line. It is important for racers to wait until the rise line above the closed gates in order to complete most of the turn above the gate. This puts the racer in position to ski a fairly straight line through the second closed gate, or ski a rounder line to prepare for an upcoming turn.

Over-hairpin

In an *into-hairpin*, the racer skis into the first closed gate (below the upper pole). Usually, the course does not have a significant rhythm change. Racers enter and exit into-hairpins in opposite directions, making one turn. The turning pole of the *second* gate (upper pole) determines the rise line and, therefore, the starting point of the turn. The placement of gates following a hairpin determines the line through the hairpin.

Into-hairpin

Flush

A flush is a vertical combination consisting of three or more closed gates. It indicates a quick change in the rhythm of the course. Racers leave a three-gate flush in the opposite direction they enter.

Flushes usually begin in the same way as over-hairpins: the racer skis over the top pole of the first closed gate. The flush should be started high enough on the rise line in order to complete the turn by the upper pole of the first gate. This positions the racer to ski a relatively straight line (shallow arc) through the second and third closed gates. Or, the racer is in position to ski a rounder line out of the second gate and entering the third gate, in order to prepare for an upcoming turn.

It is important to start the flush with a good line in order to maximize speed. If the first turn is started too early or low on the rise line, a rounder, slower line usually results.

As in an over-hairpin, course setters are inclined to set for round paths into a flush to control speed before entering fall line turns (closed gates). They tend to set for straighter paths coming out of combinations by allowing more vertical distance. This compensates for the speed gained from skiing down the fall line.

Flush

Delay Combination

A delay combination consists of an open gate, a closed or oblique gate (the delay gate) and another open gate. The purpose of the delay is to change the rhythm of the course, or to move the course to a different fall line. Delays are sometimes set to avoid an obstacle or to change to preferred terrain, for example, terrain less rutted from previous courses, or to avoid thin snow cover.

The racer should start the delay high enough on the rise line to establish the direction change necessary to continue through the closed/oblique gate. The greater distance between turns often makes it difficult to wait for the rise line of the second open gate. The point where the turn should begin above this gate is determined by the placement of gates following the delay.

For extreme direction changes, it is sometimes necessary to come-from-behind on one or both open gates of a delay combination.

The placement of the upper pole in the closed/oblique gate may not interfere with the line between open gates, or on the other hand, it can dictate the line. In the latter case, the upper pole of the delay gate becomes the turning pole. As a result, the racer may need to ski wide on the first open gate in order to be on line for the delay gate.

The delay gate is closed or oblique, whichever is more visible for the racer's direction of travel.

Delay Combination

Visual Awareness

It is essential for racers to notice upcoming gates and not just the gate in front of them. In this way, they can prepare and be ready for these gates instead of reacting to them. Have "look ahead" be a theme for training, racing and free-skiing. Visual awareness should first be developed out of the gates. Exercises for this can be found in *Technical Skills for Alpine Skiing* under the title, *Perceptual Skills*.

Course Inspection

First course inspection experiences can focus on the layout of a course by dividing it into sections, such as open gates, quick flush, open gates, long delay, knoll. Experienced racers should learn the course in greater detail, including their line in relation to course layout and terrain features. An example is, "set-up high for the 'turny' gates on the steeps...come-from-behind over the roll...sidehill turns..." The racing line should be studied especially for all difficult sections of the course. The racer should rehearse tactical strategy in his/her mind.

Whether the whole course is memorized, or just a few parts of a course are learned, it is good practice for a racer to visualize the course, or to draw it on paper, or on the snow. This activity will help the skier be more familiar with the course for when it is time to race.

Observing the rise line and exit angle will help racers to determine how "turny" different sections of the course are.

Rise Line

Exit Angle

Skiing the line

CHAPTER 4
SUPER-G and DOWNHILL

CHAPTER 4 **SUPER-G AND DOWNHILL**

Super-G and Downhill are classified as speed events, whereas Slalom and Giant Slalom are considered technical events. Training for speed events typically enhances a skier's ability to seek speed in technical events. Effective training in both is extremely valuable, even for competitors in only one category.

This chapter combines Super-G and Downhill information because these events have much in common. Both events include turns and traverses at high speed, and both require the ability to glide and the ability to adapt to terrain at high speed. In both disciplines, racers seek aerodynamic tuck positions in order to carry as much speed through the course as possible.

Aerodynamic body position

Super-G and Downhill courses consist of varying terrain including rolls, jumps, dips, and sidehill slopes, as well as long traverses and straight-aways. Although it contains characteristics common to Downhill, a Super-G course is typically described as a very fast Giant Slalom course because of the emphasis on high speed turns. Downhill courses generally use traverses, straight-aways and terrain features to a greater degree than Super-G courses do. The speed attained in Downhill is also greater than that in Super-G.

Whether a racer is free-skiing at high speeds, training for specific elements, or racing in a speed event, safety is of utmost importance. To ski safely at high speeds or in a tuck position, it is always very important for skiers to look ahead and to be prepared to slow down, or to come out of the tuck position at any time in order to avoid potentially dangerous situations. Fast skiing should be restricted to controlled training areas. Helmets that are designed specifically for Super-G and Downhill events must be worn for all fast skiing (see Chapter 5, *Equipment*). Other concerns are covered under *Safety Issues* later in this chapter.

TECHNIQUE

Turn Description

Super-G and Downhill turns are dynamic, long radius, parallel turns as summarized in Chapter 1, *Turn Technique*. The goal in every Super-G or Downhill turn is to glide in the most aerodynamic position possible. In skiing, *aerodynamic* refers to the position a skier assumes in order to cut through the air with the least amount of air resistance. *Dynamic* implies that the skier must constantly adjust his/her body position to stay in balance. *Gliding* implies carved turns in which racers maximize speed potential by using the least amount of edge angle necessary, and still remain on the best line through the gates.

Super-G and Downhill turns are typically long, high-speed, carved turns with the direction change covering a great distance. A *cross-over* movement is primarily used to edge the skis at the start of each turn. The Giant Slalom movement in which the skis cross under the body to the outside of the turn can be precarious and unpredictable at high speed. The skier's position is uncertain because the skis are momentarily weightless. Therefore, a *cross-under* movement is reserved for extreme and quick changes of direction.

The increased speeds in Super-G and Downhill turns create greater forces for the racer to withstand. As a result, angulation and a countered body position are essential in order to carve turns and maintain balance on the outside ski of the turn. In high speed turns, as in all turns, it is very important to move through a centered position during turn initiation.

Super-G and Downhill turns can be executed in an upright stance as in Giant Slalom turns, in a high tuck position with or without hands together or poles tucked under the arms, or in a low tuck position. While a low tuck position is aerodynamically most effective, it is used primarily on straight segments of the course. Elsewhere, body positions that enhance clean, carving turns are used to optimize speed. The quality of the turn is always more important than maintaining a tuck position.

Body Positions in Turns

High speed turns can be accomplished in different body positions. Racers need to be adept in all of these positions in order to meet the demands of each turn in the most aerodynamic stance. The racer strives for the most compact position possible that does not compromise the quality of the turn and the ability to stay on line. Different body positions include:
   a. Giant Slalom stance
   b. high tuck position with hands apart and forward
   c. high tuck position with hands together and poles tucked under the arms
   d. low tuck position

Body positions are not static and can be tightened or

Giant Slalom stance

extended depending on the forces the skier experiences in the turn. The greater the force, the more the skier will have to open out of the tuck in order to stay in balance. In comparison to a high tuck, a Giant Slalom stance allows for greater edge angle and body angulation to provide lateral balance. Also, the Giant Slalom position provides more rotational freedom of the upper body allowing countering movements (the outside hip is back in relation to the inside hip) to occur with angulation. This keeps the tail of the ski from skidding through the turn completion and directs the upper body toward the upcoming turn. In addition, the open arm position of Giant Slalom can assist balance.

Racers should rise out of a tuck and lower into a tuck with smooth movements since abrupt action can "catch" air and decrease speed. Whenever rising, racers should keep an aerodynamic position in mind; they should open out of a tuck with hands forward.

High tuck position, Hands apart and forward

**High tuck position,
Hands together, poles tucked under arms**

Low tuck position

Tuck Positions

Characteristics of a *low tuck* position include:
   a. Weight is centered over both feet and skis.
   b. Feet and knees are placed at an equal distance apart. The optimum distance between skis is the distance that allows the skier to maintain flat skis on the snow. It is different for each skier, depending upon the skier's anatomy and ski boot cant.
   c. The back of the skier is slightly rounded and essentially parallel to the surface of the skis. The upper leg (thigh) is nearly parallel to the ski, too, but the thigh and chest should not be in contact.
   d. Arms are held in front of the body with the elbows positioned over the outer part of the knees.
   e. Hands are held close together, with the arms either extended with a slight bend at the elbows, or bent more to bring the hands up and near the face.
   f. The head should be lifted the amount that is necessary for the skier to look ahead, down the hill.

In a *high tuck* position, the skier's legs extend into a taller position. In this position, the skier has the ability to bend and extend the legs in order to absorb abrupt changes in terrain. Arms can open forward for balance, or hands can stay together, with poles tucked under the arms.

Downhill Pole

In speed events, the racer uses the ski pole differently than in technical events. The Super-G or Downhill pole is curved to fit the skier's body for aerodynamic purposes. The pole is seldom planted during a speed event since this action would create air friction. When a ski pole *is* planted in Super-G or Downhill, the movements are the same as for Giant Slalom.

Low tuck position

Low tuck position

High tuck position

High tuck position

SKILL DEVELOPMENT

Safety Prerequisites

A strong base of well-rounded technical skills is essential before a skier is ready to reach the speeds attained in speed events. Before allowing skiers to train for Super-G or Downhill, they must master the following skills.

  a. Safety Stop

   Racers absolutely must be able to come to a relatively quick stop from a fast speed. Teach a safety stop from a straight run, starting in a tall stance. The skier quickly drops to a lower position in order to pivot the skis into a sideslip. This slows the skier's speed. Then, increasing the edge angle brings the skier to a stop. A safety stop from a tuck position should be practiced, too, where the skier rises into an upright stance before pivoting the skis.

Straight run

Safety Stop

b. Balance on the Outside Ski

Before skiing at high speeds, skiers must be able to demonstrate their ability to balance on the outside ski in every turn. Otherwise the outside ski may bang against the snow and bounce off at high speeds. As a practice exercise, have skiers lift the inside ski of the turn. In this way, the outside ski will stay weighted and completely control the arc of the turn.

Lift the inside ski exercise

c. Arms in Front

Skiers must be able to keep their arms in front of their bodies in order to maintain a balanced position. They should be able to turn without swinging or planting their ski poles, or dragging their poles for balance.

d. Look Ahead

Skiers must be able to look far enough down the hill to quickly decide their line through terrain, courses, and around obstacles.

Exercises to refine these prerequisites can be found in Chapter 3 of this book, and they are further developed in *Technical Skills for Alpine Skiing*.

Arms in Front

Look Ahead

Adjusting to Longer Skis

Longer skis provide stability for Super-G and Downhill events. Determining the appropriate ski length is discussed under *Speed Events* in Chapter 5. It is important for racers to free-ski on their Downhill skis as often as possible before racing. For skiers to feel comfortable and confident on a longer ski, first review the safety prerequisites: safety stop, balance on the outside ski, hands in front, and look ahead. They should practice dynamic turns, while increasing the turn radius and speed of descent on smooth terrain. They should build from Giant Slalom to Super-G and Downhill turns. As skill level allows, have skiers progress to variable terrain. Whenever possible, they should ski at a comfortable speed in different snow conditions to experience hard-packed snow, ice, crud and powder. Exercises to adjust to longer skis include these:

Hop turns

a. Hop turns are very beneficial in helping skiers "feel" the tips and tails of their longer skis. Skiers should be able to link rhythmic hop turns on flat and steep terrain. Make sure the skiers land on and hop off edges without skidding out.

b. Have skiers practice turning without their ski poles. Encourage them to focus their attention on their feet in order to feel the ski's edge and the transfer of weight from ski to ski.

Ski Pole Action

A pole plant is not used for most high speed turns. Instead, hands are held in front of the body in an aerodynamic position. On very steep or "turny" sections of a course, the pole swing and plant/touch may be necessary for stability, or to help direct the body into the upcoming turn. When a ski pole *is* planted in Super-G or Downhill, the movements are the same as for Giant Slalom. Exercises include:

Skiing without poles

a. Have skiers ski a series of turns on intermediate terrain, progressing to a steep slope. Have them use a pole swing and touch to experience this action with a Downhill pole.

b. Have skiers ski a series of turns without swinging or planting the poles.

Many racers develop the habit of dragging their poles when they are not in a tuck position. Have skiers practice keeping the poles from touching the snow so as not to depend on them for balance.

61

Flat Ski Exercises

To glide, racers must use only the degree of edge necessary to stay on line. Since skiing on a flat ski is faster than on an edged ski, and less edge is faster than more edge, it is important to develop edge awareness. Exercises:

a. Have skiers glide straight down a gentle hill while in an upright balanced stance, with feet comfortably apart. Have them feel for flat skis on the snow. To feel the difference between flat and edged skis, they can experiment by tipping onto right and then left edges. They should also explore tipping onto both inside and both outside edges.

b. Examine ski tracks left in the snow to determine if the skis are flat.

c. Two skiers start side-by-side in upright stances. As they glide straight down a gentle hill, each skier tries to pull ahead of the other by maintaining flatter skis on the snow. This race can also be used to compare ski waxes.

d. With a partner, the leader carves turns at a consistent radius and speed. While skiing in the leader's tracks, the follower experiments with using as little edge as necessary to stay close to the leader.

Tuck Position Exercises

Introduce high and low tucks in a static position, and have skiers practice at slow speeds at first. Video feedback can be very helpful for shaping a skier's optimum position.

Straight Run Tuck Exercises

Have skiers perform the following tasks from a balanced position, gliding straight in the fall line. Remind skiers to rise out of, and lower into, a tuck position with smooth movements. It is also important to open out of a tuck with hands and arms in a forward position. Have skiers practice safety stops after each exercise.
   a. In a low tuck, shift weight from foot to foot.
   b. In a high tuck, step skis up and down.
   c. In a low tuck, rock forward toward the ski tips and rock backward, toward the ski tails; find a centered position.
   d. Alternate a low tuck position with an upright stance.
   e. Alternate an upright stance with a high tuck position.

Feel for flat skis

Wax race

f. Alternate low tuck, upright stance, and high tuck positions.
g. Alternate low and high tuck positions.
h. Alternate low and high tuck positions with exercises that are performed in an upright stance, such as, march from foot to foot, shuffle feet, hop on one or both skis.

Traverse Exercises

A countered and angulated position is necessary to maintain edge hold in a traverse. Have skiers travel across the hill in a low or high tuck position with skis tipped onto uphill edges. The skis should track, and not skid or slip sideways, losing the edge. Have skiers assume a position in which the uphill side of the body and the uphill ski are slightly ahead. Their upper body should turn to face slightly down the hill, while their shoulders stay level. Have skiers perform the following exercises while traversing across the hill:
   a. Over-edge and under-edge the skis to explore different degrees of edging. Too much edge will result in the skis curving up the hill. Not enough edge will result in slipping down the hill. Find the minimum degree of edge necessary to stay on a designated line.
   b. Alternate a low tuck with an upright stance.
   c. Alternate a high tuck with an upright stance.
   d. Alternate low and high tuck positions.

Also, have skiers practice traverses across small-to-medium sized bumps in a high tuck position. To maintain ski/snow contact, skiers should rock forward and press the tips of the skis down the back, steep side of the bumps. They should absorb terrain with the legs, keeping the upper body relatively quiet.

Turn Exercises

The following wedge and parallel exercises help to develop edging skills in turns:

   a. Wedge Edge Locks

   This exercise develops the feel of edging and over-edging the skis. From a gliding wedge at slow speed on gentle terrain, have skiers greatly increase the edging angle of one ski to move in the direction this "railed" ski travels. Have them release the edge by flattening the ski, and then greatly increasing the edge of the other ski, to move in the direction it points.

Tuck traverse

Wedge Edge Locks

b. Carved Wedge Turns

Carved wedge turns can be used as an exercise to teach hip angulation and to feel edging movements better. Have skiers begin with medium radius wedge turns moving at a slow speed on gentle terrain. While maintaining the wedge position, have them gradually increase their speed and the radius of their turns. It is important to feel edging movements along the inside of the foot. They should focus on carved turns, feeling the inside edge of the outside ski as it cuts through the snow.

Carved Wedge Turns

The skier's body position in a wedge turn creates an angle above the skier's hip. The upper body stays vertical while the lower body is at a slant to the snow. This position, called hip angulation, is a strong position that relies on skeletal alignment from the foot to the hip for support. In high speed parallel turns, the outside ski maintains a hip angulated position as exhibited in the wedge position.

c. Parallel Edge Locks

In this exercise, the sidecut of the edged and weighted ski gradually draws an arc in the snow. Have skiers tip both skis onto right edges and weight the left, outside ski while gliding down a gentle slope. Then, have them tip both skis onto left edges and weight the right, outside ski. They should not steer the skis.

Parallel Edge Locks

d. High-Speed Parallel Turns

In this maneuver, look for a hip-angulated position in which the skier's upper body is vertical and his/her shoulders are level, creating an angle above the hip. Have skiers perform large radius, dynamic, parallel turns. As in the wedge turns, have them focus on the inside edge of the outside foot/ski as it cuts arcs through the snow.

High-Speed Parallel Turns

Transitions Between Turns

Not only the turns but also the transitions between them can be accomplished in different positions. Have skiers practice the following transition exercises moving smoothly, but deliberately, through positions:

a. Have skiers ski in a low tuck position during transitions between turns that are performed in a Giant Slalom stance. They should *open forward* out of the low tuck at the start of the turn. It is important for the racer's hands, arms and body to move forward, and not up and back, as he/she opens out of the tuck position. The moment the direction change in the turn is complete, skiers should drop into a low tuck position bringing the hands together and the ski poles under the arms.

Resuming the tuck position too early in the turn will flatten the skis' edge angle on the snow and can cause the skis to skid. Waiting too long before resuming the tuck position will reduce the speed.

b. Have skiers ski in a low tuck position during transitions between high tuck turns. They should open forward into the high tuck as described above. Hands stay apart, and forward; hands are not out to the skier's sides.

To carve the turn in a high tuck position, have skiers focus on a slightly countered, angulated position, keeping the shoulders level.

c. Have skiers ski in a low tuck position during transitions between high tuck turns. In the turn, they should maintain the body movement described in (b.) but with hands together, and ski poles tucked under the arms throughout the turn.

In the Air

There is the potential to become airborne over rolls, bumps, jumps, or knolls particularly in Downhill events. The objective should be to maintain ski/snow contact or, when that is not possible, to get back on the snow quickly. It is faster to glide on the snow than fly through the air. There are three techniques that are used to adapt to these terrain changes.

A *press* is most often used over relatively smooth terrain transitions. This movement provides stability if the racer leaves the snow, and minimizes time in the air. Instruct the racer to press his/her hands down and forward toward the ski binding toe-pieces. This movement helps the racer to project his/her upper body forward until it is perpendicular to the angle of the downslope. The hand movement assists the skier in assuming an aerodynamic tuck position in flight.

A *pre-jump* should be reserved for more abrupt terrain changes. The racer leaves the snow before the terrain change to avoid, for example, the "lip" on a knoll. He/she quickly retracts his/her legs into an aerodynamic tuck position to clear the lip. In this way, he/she actually jumps over the lip. This pre-jump allows the racer to land on the snow sooner than otherwise possible. To absorb the impact of landing, the racer extends his/her legs just before contacting the surface of the snow.

Jumps allow racers to avoid bumpy, uneven, or rolling terrain. An example is jumping from the uphill side of one roll to land on the downhill side of a second roll, thereby skipping the terrain between the rolls. To lift off the snow, the racer extends, projecting his/her body forward until it is perpendicular to the angle of the downslope. Immediately after the extension, he/she should lift the legs into an aerodynamic tuck position, and then extend the legs to absorb the impact upon landing.

These terrain elements require much practice in order to time the movements correctly, especially at high speeds. Large rolls can be built to practice all three actions. Some racers find it helpful to "make their move" as their ski tips reach the lip in a press or jump, or as they reach the lift-off point for a pre-jump. In this way, they adjust their reaction time in relation to their speed of descent.

DRILLS

Terrain Courses

Terrain courses provide a wonderfully challenging environment for skiers to explore balance, learn about ski/snow contact, and focus on a smooth flow of movement down the hill.

Build rolls, bumps, pedal pumps, banked turns, knolls and ridges. These features can be built with snow grooming equipment. Work with the staff of the slope maintenance department to set up a course.

Have skiers use leg action to absorb variations in terrain as they keep their hands in front for balance. They should rock forward and press the ski tips down the steep side of rolls, bumps, and knolls, to move the upper body down the hill and to maintain ski/snow contact.

Banked turns and ridges require good balance on the outside ski as both skis are guided through the turn.

To jump safely, it is essential for skiers to look ahead to the landing and be sure it is clear of people or obstacles. Skiers should jump from a balanced position with ankles and knees flexed, ready to spring. The skier should project the upper body in an upward and forward direction while extending the legs to lift off the jump. Hands should be positioned in front for stability. For the landing, a fairly tall stance is important so the legs can bend to absorb the impact.

Course Elements

Course elements, such as turns, traverses, rolls, and jumps can be practiced separately. Vary the terrain to provide the skiers with different experiences. Then gradually add elements together to create longer courses.

Terrain course

COURSE DESCRIPTION

Regulations and dimensions in this section are derived from the International Ski Federation (FIS) rule book, *The International Ski Competition Rules*. The origin (article number) of each quote is noted in parenthesis.

Terrain Features

Super-G courses are set on "undulating and hilly" terrain whenever possible (1002.1). Rolls, dips, sidehill slopes and jumps are common terrain features.

Downhill courses cover varying terrain over a long distance. Terrain features may include steep and flat pitches, banked turns and sidehills, long traverses, rolls, dips, bumps and the "natural unevenness of the ground" (702.3).

Gate Dimensions

Each Super-G or Downhill gate consists of four poles and two panels, as drawn. Men's Downhill courses contain only red, or "luminous orange" colored gates. Men's and women's Super-G courses, and women's Downhill courses alternate red and blue colored gates.

The corresponding diagram shows the dimensions of Super-G and Downhill gates. In Super-G, "The distance between the turning poles of two successive gates must be at least 25 meters." (1003.1.2).

Course Description

Super-G and Downhill courses consist of open, closed, and oblique gates. The gate panels must be set at right angles to the racing line for visibility. In both speed events, a *corridor*, consisting of two open gates, is commonly set to designate one turn. For a detailed description and diagram of a corridor, look under *Super-G and Downhill Tactics*.

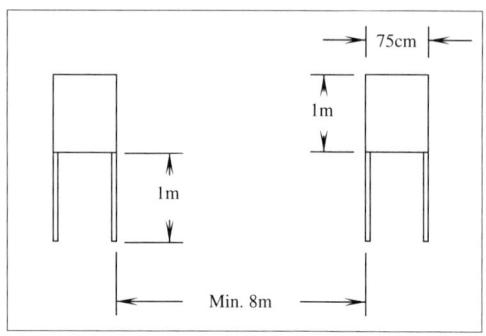

Downhill Gate Dimensions

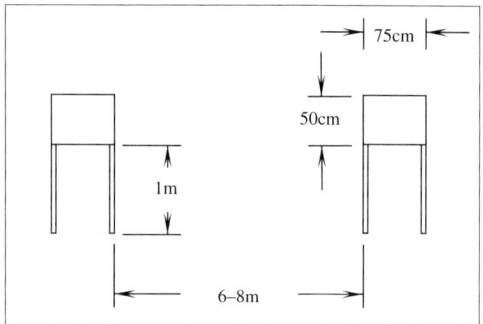

Super-G Gate Dimensions

Course Drawing

Course inspection and official training runs are required prior to every Downhill race. During this time, the racer learns the layout of the course in conjunction with terrain features, and the racing line through the course. It is important to establish names for every turn or section of the course in order for the athletes and coaches to communicate accurately.

Immediately after course inspection, or the initial training run, have racers draw as much of the course as they remember. This small scale representation of the course should be drawn to show relative distances between gates as well as gate placement. Have the racers label each gate by name and note the terrain. Finally, have the racers draw their line through the course. This exercise will help racers learn the course.

After the first training day, review the drawings with each athlete. This will indicate to the coach and athlete if there is a lack of understanding. The coach can draw and describe any missed or incorrect sections of the course. Have the athlete study the drawing and then visualize the course several times.

Have athletes re-draw the course following the second day of training. Have athletes draw the rise line and exit angle for each gate. Use these lines as a basis for drawing the racing line. Coaches can refer to their notes taken on-the-hill to show, on the athletes' drawings, where the athlete can alter his/her line, or change position in order to gain speed. These suggestions may include changes such as skiing a tighter or wider line, starting a turn lower or higher above a gate, or lowering into a tuck sooner.

The characteristics of a race hill often require course setters to set a similar course for every Downhill event. Therefore, encourage athletes to keep their drawings for future review. Coaches should also keep a record of the course to prepare for the next race at that location.

The adjacent example of course drawing is taken from an actual drawing by a thirteen-year-old at his first Downhill event.

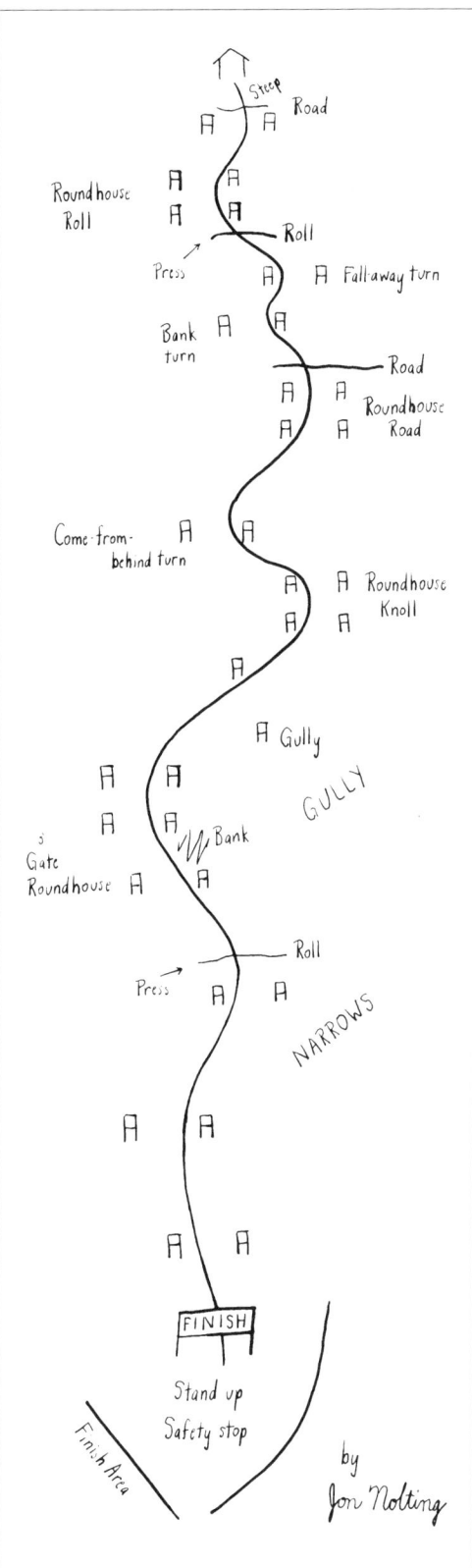

Course Drawing by Jon Nolting

SUPER-G AND DOWNHILL TACTICS

The material presented in Chapter 1, *Giant Slalom Tactics*, forms the basis for Super-G and Downhill tactics.

Tactics

Super-G and Downhill turns have a much larger radius than Giant Slalom turns. They are performed at higher speeds, and cover more distance down the hill. As a result, racers generally start Super-G and Downhill turns much higher on the rise line in comparison to Giant Slalom tactics.

Although the turning poles in Downhill indicate the racing line, they are so far apart that they may not designate specific turning points. The fastest line may not pass just below each gate, as is usually the case in Giant Slalom courses. Depending on the set of the upcoming gates, a lower line may actually be faster.

Super-G and Downhill Tactics

Although the general line through a course is similar for all racers, the specific line for each individual racer may need to be modified. The determining factors for individual line include the skier's skill level, strength, and speed of travel. An experienced racer, for example, who can ski a tighter (closer) line to a gate can start the turn comparatively lower on the rise line than a less capable racer.

It is important to note that the optimum line for each individual may change with each training or race run due to increased speed from tighter, aerodynamic body positioning. As the skier's speed increases, the line becomes wider in order to make direction changes at the greater speed.

Course conditions can also have a dramatic impact on line. A course with new fallen snow, for example, may run slower, and therefore require a close (tight) line. In another example, a course on a cloudy day may run faster than on the previous sunny, warm day, and therefore require an open (wide) line.

Corridor

A corridor consists of two or three open gates that are set to designate one long turn. The lower gate is positioned directly below (a), or slightly off-set (b) and (c) in relation to the upper gate. The placements of the lower gate and the gate following the corridor determine the line through the upper gate. The line can vary considerably as shown in the diagrams.

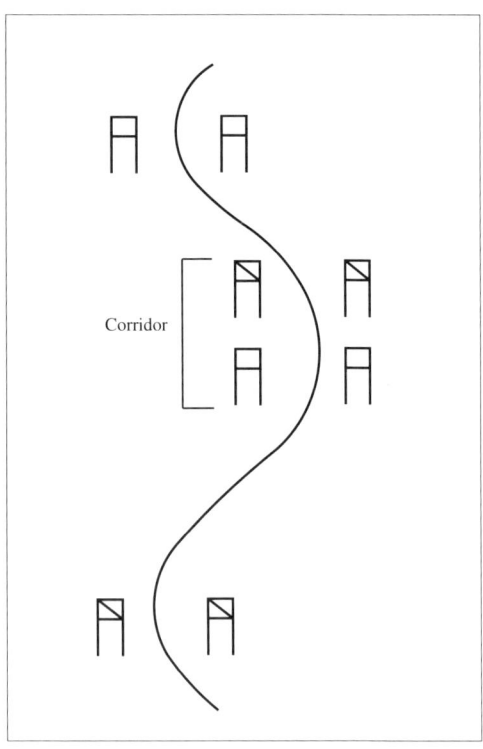

(a) Corridor–Lower gate directly below

The gate count for Super-G includes only those gates which require a direction change. Therefore, in the total count, a corridor is considered to be one gate.

Course Inspection

The goal in course inspection is to memorize the course in order to anticipate gate placement and terrain features while traveling at high speeds (see *Giant Slalom Tactics*). It is important to be able to visualize, describe, and draw the course in order to understand fully its design and demands.

Training Run Strategy

Super-G, like Giant Slalom, does not allow for training runs prior to the event. Only course inspection is held.

In Downhill, three days are usually scheduled for course inspection and official training prior to the race. Two training days, or at least two training runs, must take place. One of these runs must be timed. Complete course inspection takes place before the first training run.

As in Giant Slalom (see Chapter 2), have racers visualize the course after inspection. Give a verbal start command for them to leave the start and race the course in their minds. The amount of time it takes to "ski" the visualized course should be similar to their actual skiing time.

Course drawing is described in detail earlier in this chapter under the heading, *Course Description*. Courses can be drawn on paper while riding the lift, or in the snow while waiting at the start.

The objectives in the following run sequence are appropriate for a racer's first Downhill experiences. It is especially suitable for training at home. If tactical or technical problems arise, the racer should address the problem(s) specific to that section of the course before advancing to a more demanding situation.
  a. First Run
    Ski in a Giant Slalom position ("stand-up run") and concentrate on the correct line to become familiar with the course, and to gain confidence.
  b. Second Run
    Ski in a lower stance and tuck between turns at appropriate times.
  c. Third Run
    Ski in the lowest position possible, never sacrificing the quality of a turn for a low body position. Slightly

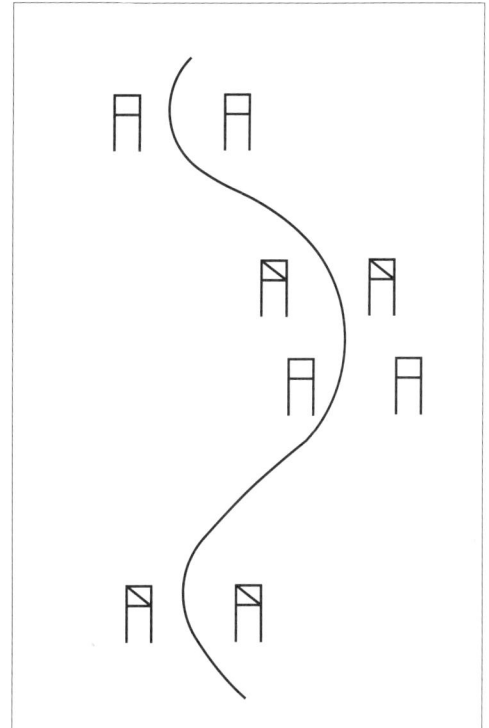

(b) Corridor–Lower gate off-set

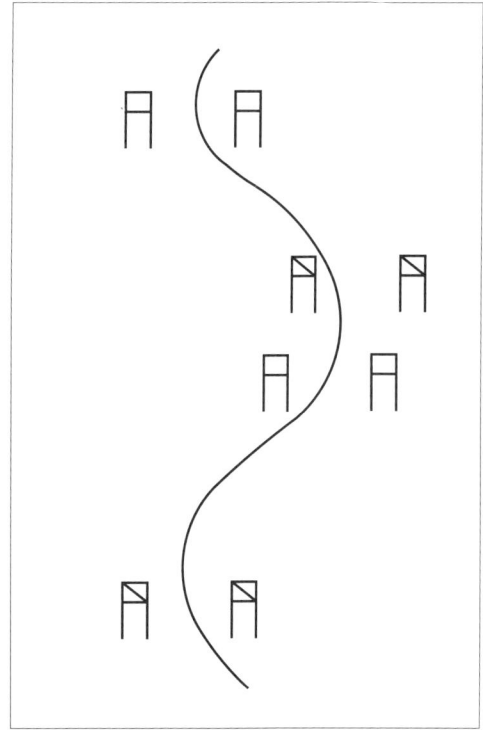

(c) Corridor–Lower gate off-set

widen the line in the turns to compensate for higher speeds.
   d. Fourth Run
      The fourth run is a race rehearsal. Concentrate on speed and fine-tuning the line.

In an actual race situation, four training runs are often reduced to two runs due to weather and course conditions. With adequate preparation prior to an actual event, racers should be ready, following a thorough course inspection, to ski aggressively starting with their first training run.

Coaches should be positioned along the course to cover the whole course, or, if not possible, to cover the crucial parts. Coaches should write notes for reference and then speak to each athlete about his/her performance before the next training run. Look for correct technique and tactics.

SPEED EVENT SAFETY

The element of speed in Super-G and Downhill necessitates safety measures. Athletes must be made aware of the greater danger involved in these events. Downhill racers do not take risks to ski fast, they ski technically and tactically well.

Readiness Criteria

Skiers must be capable of the following requirements before training or racing in speed events. Refer to *Safety Prerequisites* under *Skill Development* in this chapter for descriptions of (a.–c.)
   a. balance on the outside ski
   b. look ahead
   c. stop with a safety stop
   d. stay focused and follow directions. Athletes who forget directions, perform unpredictably, or are easily distracted, cannot be relied on to make safe judgments at high speed.

Helmets

Coaches should require racers to wear well-fitting helmets that are specifically designed for Super-G and Downhill events. Helmets that meet European safety standards (currently, there is no helmet standard in the United States) should be used. These helmets are reinforced with fiberglass and kevlar, and therefore, provide greater protection than plastic helmets in high speed impacts. Detailed information, including sizing and safety features of models for all disciplines, is contained in Chapter 5, and in the *Appendix*.

Free-skiing

Racers should always ski a hill at Giant Slalom speed before skiing at a faster speed. This provides the racer with an opportunity to assess the terrain and snow conditions before increasing speed. Fast skiing should be restricted to controlled training areas. Skiers must learn not to come close to another person, the edge of a trail, or an object such as a sign, lift tower, or snow-making machinery, etc. If a fall should occur, enough space between the skier and potential obstacles must be allowed in order to come to a stop without a collision.

Racers should ski at a very slow speed when they practice tuck positions on long, gently sloping roads or "cat walks". They should stay away from the edge of the road in case they "catch an edge" and slide off the road. Even when practicing a tuck at slow speeds, skiers should stand upright whenever they ski close to another skier.

The loss of a ski at high speed is potentially very dangerous. Skiers should be told to lean over and fall on their side in order to slide to a stop. They should not attempt to recover on one ski.

In the Course

If a ski comes off during a training or racing run, the skier should immediately fall, as described in the previous paragraph.

While traveling at high speeds, "hitting" a gate will reduce speed and can dangerously knock a skier off balance.

Yellow Zone

The *yellow zone* is a designated location on a Downhill course at which racers are required to stop to avoid a dangerous situation located below that point. At a yellow zone, an official waves a yellow flag to signal the racer to come to a stop. The racer uses a safety stop to slow down and stop. In a race, the competitor should then go directly to the start for a re-run, and not ski the rest of the course. During training runs, the racer must ask a member of the jury permission to continue down the course.

Stopping Safely

Racers should use a safety stop to come to a stop after crossing the finish line. Teach skiers to rise out of their tuck position immediately in preparation for stopping. After coming to a complete stop, the skier must leave the finish area so it is clear for the next racer. These actions should always be upheld while training or racing to avoid accidents. Some racers tend to stop thinking the moment they cross the finish line. Teach racers that the run is not over until they leave the finish area.

CHAPTER 5
EQUIPMENT

CHAPTER 5 **EQUIPMENT**

This chapter includes information concerning head protection for all events and safety equipment specifically for Slalom and Giant Slalom. Ski length for the speed events is also discussed.

SAFETY EQUIPMENT

Slalom and Giant Slalom

In Giant Slalom, *arm pads* protect racers from contact with the turning pole. They are helpful for racers who have not learned to "hand clear" Slalom flex poles, but ski close enough to the pole for arm contact. This is the same action as "brushing" a bamboo pole, for which arm pads are also beneficial.

Pole guards are important in Slalom for protecting the hands when clearing Slalom poles. They consist of a plastic strip that attaches around the ski pole grip and extends over the hand.

Shin guards protect the lower legs when contact with Slalom poles occurs. The guards are made of plastic and attach with straps around the racer's legs.

Face guards keep goggles in place and protect the face from contact with Slalom poles. They typically consist of a visor, a bar that extends in front of the racer's mouth, and a strap that fits around the head to secure the guard in place.

Goggles should always be worn to protect the eyes when skiing in a training or race course.

See the following information regarding helmets. Further information can be found in the *Appendix*.

Helmets for All Events

Helmets provide head protection while free-skiing, training, or racing. It is important to use the appropriate model for its intended use. Giant Slalom helmets are also appropriate for all-day wear. This model is lightweight, low in profile, and has a hard plastic shell. It can be modified for Slalom with a bar attachment for deflecting poles and a visor for added eye protection. Super-G and Downhill helmet shells are reinforced with fiberglass and kevlar. A jaw protector can be attached to these helmets for added protection of the face and teeth.

It is extremely important for helmets to be sized correctly. The correct size can be determined by measuring the head circumference (in inches or centimeters) and then referring to the manufacturer's sizing chart. Padding can be added to ensure a snug and comfortable fit. A helmet that is too large will not be as effective in preventing injury because the head can hit the inside of the helmet upon impact. For a child, a too large helmet can be too heavy.

It is necessary to position the strap under the chin for a secure fit. A helmet should be worn without a hat underneath. The liner of the helmet provides the warmth of a hat. Helmets are available with a small opening at the ear that does not disturb hearing or balance.

Sizes ranging from very small helmets for children to adult XXL are available.

In the *Appendix*, a detailed article explains answers to questions such as: Do helmets decrease the risk of injury? Do helmets restrict hearing and vision? Are helmets practical for all-day use?

SPEED EVENTS

At high speeds, longer skis are necessary for stability. Downhill skis are generally longer than Super-G skis. Super-G and Downhill poles are used to reduce aerodynamic drag.

Ski Length

Young racers can be introduced to Super-G and Downhill events using Giant Slalom skis and poles. The deeper sidecut of Slalom skis make them inappropriate for speed events. If a skier is accustomed to using a Slalom ski for the technical events, then a Giant Slalom ski of the same length should be substituted for speed events. In general, an increase in ski length should not exceed ten centimeters for young racers (J3 and younger) or for racers that have few speed event experiences. The determining factor when selecting a longer ski is the racer's ability to bend the ski successfully through the arc of a turn.

When young skiers choose skis which are five-to-ten centimeters longer for speed events, they should consider a ski which they can grow into for Giant Slalom in the future.

For young skiers, the transition from a junior ski to an adult ski is significant and should be considered when increasing ski length. A ski designed for adults can be too stiff, such that a junior racer cannot exert force to bend it into a circular arc for carved turns.

Highly skilled racers have many variables to consider when selecting the appropriate length Super-G or Downhill skis. Physical attributes (size, strength, skill), as well as the technical characteristics of the ski, such as the sidecut, and the turn and speed elements of courses to be raced, all play decisive roles. Once again, the major determining factor is the racer's ability to bend the ski throughout the turn.

At times, Giant Slalom skis are more appropriate for a "turny" Super-G, and Super-G skis will be better suited for a "turny" Downhill. The demands of the turns generally provide the determining factor when choosing a Giant Slalom, Super-G or Downhill ski for a specific course.

Ski Poles

Straight ski poles can inhibit skiers from achieving their optimal tuck position. Downhill and Super-G poles are curved to fit around the skier while in a tuck. Skiers who have helmets with jaw protectors should wear their helmets when selecting poles. The ski pole may need a slightly different bend so that the helmet does not interfere with pole position while in a tuck.

CHAPTER 6
RACE PROCEDURES

CHAPTER 6 **RACE PROCEDURES**

START AND FINISH PROCEDURES

Timing

The timer starts when the starting wand is pushed open from contact with the racer's legs. It stops when the racer intersects, or "breaks" the light beam across the finish.

Start Command

The start command for Slalom is: "Ready", followed a few seconds later by, "Go!" The competitor must start within about 10 seconds of this command (805.3).

The start command for Giant Slalom, Super-G and Downhill is: "Ten Seconds", and then five seconds later, "5,4,3,2,1, Go". The racer can leave the start within five seconds before, or five seconds after the signal (word), "Go".

Start Position

Positioned in the start, the racer's body and skis should aim toward the outside of the first gate. He/she should stand close behind the wand without touching it. The ski poles should be placed over the wand and planted securely in the snow. When the start command is given, the racer leads with the upper body to gain momentum down the hill before the wand opens. The racer should aggressively rock forward and straighten the arms to project the upper body down the hill. Then, he/she should pull down and back with the arms to pull the legs through, opening the wand with the lower leg(s). The steeper the hill out of the start, the more the ski tips need to be pushed down (or heels lifted) to match the angle of the slope. After leaving the start, the racer can choose to pole or skate toward the first gate. He/she should allow enough time to weight the outside ski, in position for the first turn, before reaching the first gate.

Leaving the start

Racers should practice starting from different locations to gain varied experience.

To have racers practice leaving the start and preparing for the first gate, set two gates following a start location. Repeatedly time each racer to the second gate. Encourage racers to improve their time with each start. The placement of the two gates can be varied to direct racers to set up for different lines.

Finish Position

In Giant Slalom, the racer is generally in a low position or a tuck position after the last gate approaching the finish. From this position, the racer can choose to thrust his/her hands down and forward to "cut" the light beam.

The finish position for Slalom depends on the distance from the last gate to the finish line and the racer's speed of descent. He/she skates, poles, or tucks in an aggressive effort to reach the finish as fast as possible.

In Super-G and Downhill the racer stays in a tuck until crossing the finish.

Come to a Stop

As stated in Chapter 4, *Speed Event Safety*, instantly after crossing the finish, racers should slow down and come to a full stop using a safety stop. When finishing in a tuck position, teach racers to rise immediately out of their tuck in preparation for stopping.

Clear the Finish

After coming to a complete stop, the racer must leave the finish area so it is clear for the next racer. This action should always be upheld whether training or racing to avoid collisions. Some racers tend to stop thinking the moment they cross the finish line. Teach racers that the run is not over until they come to a stop and leave the finish area.

COURSE SETTING

Technical Data

A Slalom or Giant Slalom race consists of the combined time of two runs on two different courses. A Super-G or Downhill race consists of one run. Technical data regarding the number of gates and vertical drop required for FIS (International Ski Federation) races can be found in section 900 for Giant Slalom, 800 Slalom, 1000 for Super-G, and 700 for Downhill in the *International Ski Competition Rules* (FIS Rule Book). The origin (article number) of information or quotes is noted in parenthesis.

Course Setter Responsibilities

The following criteria were established by the *United States*

Ski Coaches Association for the purpose of evaluating courses. The course setter is responsible for setting a course which:

    a. is safe
    b. is legal
    c. is rhythmic and flowing
    d. is appropriate for the ability level of the skiers
    e. uses the available terrain effectively

Courses should be set so that all competitors can ski them; gates should not be set to trick racers.

When considering the safety aspects of a course, take into account the path in which a skier is likely to fall. The path should be clear of obstacles and away from precipitous slopes. Always allow a margin for error so that racers will slide to a stop without hitting an object in the event of falls.

Measure Distances

Specific gate dimensions for each discipline are diagrammed under *Course Description* within each chapter. Ski length can be used as a tool to measure these distances and determine gate placement. For example, two to three ski lengths of a 200 cm ski (two meters) will position the inside and outside poles of a gate four–six meters apart. A line designating 0.75 meter can be marked on the skis to measure the distance between closed gates of a vertical combination.

When the gates are set in the snow, make sure they are vertical, and not set at a slant. The base of a flex pole must be below the snow surface and the hinge above the surface in order for the pole to bend when hit.

For USSA or FIS races, the referee will ask the course setter for a count of the total number of gates in the course. It is helpful to ask an assistant to keep track of the numbers.

Ski the Hill

Before setting a course, ski the hill to gain a general understanding of the terrain and a specific grasp of terrain fluctuations. Observe transitions in pitch, changes in trail direction/fall line, sidehills, rolls, bumps, ruts, etc. Pre-visualize the course considering the existing terrain factors.

In Giant Slalom and Super-G races, gates "...must not be set down the fall line of the slope. The full width of a hill should be used whenever possible." (903.1.3)

Open Gates

Open gates are set perpendicular to the fall line. In setting a consistent rhythm with open gates, it is helpful to determine a point down the hill to aim toward. Then, draw an imaginary line to that point. Off-set poles at an equal distance from the imaginary line. Keep vertical distances the same. After setting the first four gates, set the following gates in line with these gates to maintain the rhythm.

Closed Gates

Closed gates are vertical gates that can be set singularly, or together for gate combinations. Panels are narrower in order to distinguish closed gates from open gates in Giant Slalom, Super-G, and Downhill events.

Oblique Gates

Oblique gates are used in all four disciplines. An oblique gate is set diagonally to the fall line. The outside pole is set at an angle down the hill in relation to the inside pole, instead of horizontally across. This is done to change the appearance of the course, to indicate an upcoming gate combination or change in rhythm, or to fit the outside pole in a narrow section.

Set the inside turning pole first. Then set the outside pole in line with the inside pole of the same gate, and the outside pole of the previous gate (if an open gate).

Rhythm Sections

Following are examples of when to set rhythmical gates:
 a. Set open gates out of the start to allow the skier to develop a rhythm. The method described in *Open Gates* can be used to establish the rhythm.
 b. Set a rhythmical section of open gates before and after gate combinations to enhance the flow of the course.
 c. At the end of a course, establish a rhythm with open gates set close to the fall line. At this point skiers may be tired. This is not the place to add required gate combinations.

Rhythm enhances flow

Changes in Rhythm

Course setters change the rhythm of a course to add variety, to test the versatility of the racer, and to adapt the course to different terrain features.

Rhythm changes can be accomplished by setting open gates or gate combinations. By varying the placement of open gates, the rhythm and speed of the course will change. When both the vertical and horizontal distances are moved, the speed of descent will either increase, decrease, or stay the same.
- a. Speed increases when gates are set closer to the fall line
- b. Speed decreases when gates are set farther from the fall line
- c. Speed decreases when the vertical distance between gates is decreased
- d. Speed increases when the vertical distance between gates is increased

Quick rhythm change

Gate combinations, such as an over-hairpin or flush in Slalom, require quick direction changes in the fall line and therefore, quick rhythm changes. In a delay, the length of one turn is extended, causing a change in the rhythm of the course.

Changes in Pitch

Changes in the pitch of a slope typically dictate the following changes in a course:
- a. On steep slopes, set a rounder course by placing gates more across the hill to control speed. A "turny" course can also be accomplished by *decreasing* the vertical distance between gates, or by a combination of both methods (horizontal and vertical placement).
- b. On flat sections of the hill, set a "straighter" course by placing gates closer to the fall line in order to carry speed. A faster course can also be accomplished by *increasing* the vertical distance between gates, or by a combination of both methods.
- c. To encourage smooth transitions, gradually change the set of the course over the distance of a few gates to lead into the change of pitch.

Hairpin

A minimum of three hairpins is required in a FIS Slalom course. The hairpins can be over-hairpins or into-hairpins or a combination thereof (803.2).

An *over-hairpin* can be set just for the purpose of altering rhythm, or with the intention of changing the skier's position on the hill. The skier's line in a hairpin is much the same as in a garland exercise (*Technical Skills for Alpine Skiing* Level 4). Since the skier exits in the same direction the hairpin is entered, the skier travels across the hill. This may be necessary to avoid the ruts from a previous course, or an obstacle, or to move to different terrain, or to redirect the skier's line a few gates before the finish.

The upper pole of the first closed gate of the hairpin can be set as if it were another open gate placed to continue the rhythm of the course. Finish setting this gate and the second closed gate of the hairpin. The position of the upper pole of the second closed gate determines the placement of the gate following the hairpin.

Racers enter and exit *into-hairpins* in opposite directions making one turn. First, set the lower pole of the upper closed gate to dictate the turn though the hairpin. Then set the upper pole and second closed gate. The position of the upper pole of the second closed gate determines the placement of the gate following the hairpin.

With this method of setting, the course should stay rhythmic. The racer will naturally ski into the hairpin and not confuse it with an over-hairpin. An into-hairpin should not disrupt the flow of the course.

Flush

In a FIS course, "...a minimum of one and a maximum of three vertical combinations consisting of three to four gates..." are required (803.2). These vertical combinations, called flushes, are usually three gates long.

Flushes are generally set on the flatter terrain of a course because they have the potential to generate a great increase in speed.

A flush indicates a quick change in rhythm. Flushes usually begin in the same way as over-hairpins: the racer skis above the top pole of the first closed gate. In this way, racers leave a three-gate flush in the opposite direction they enter.

Set for a rounder line into a flush to control speed before entering fall line turns (closed gates). Coming out of the flush, set gates closer to the fall line, and/or increase the vertical distance to compensate for the speed gained from skiing down the fall line. The position of the upper pole of the third closed gate determines the set of the gate following the flush.

Delay Combination

A delay combination consists of an open gate, a closed or oblique gate (the delay gate) and another open gate. Set a delay combination to change the rhythm of the course, or to move the course to a different fall line. Use delay combinations to avoid an obstacle, to move to terrain less rutted from previous courses, or to avoid thin snow cover.

The distance between the two open gates of a delay combination is generally greater than the distance between other open gates in the course. It is helpful to set the open gates of the combination first and then go back and set the delay gate. The delay combination dictates an extended change of direction across the hill. Therefore, set for a straighter line into and out of the delay combination in order to continue the flow of the course.

The delay gate should be set perpendicular to the racer's line of travel to make it more visible to the racer. The upper pole of the delay gate may not interfere with the line between the open gates or, on the other hand, it can be set to dictate the line. In the latter case, the upper pole of the delay gate becomes the turning pole instead of the open gate above. As a result, the racer may need to ski wide on the first open gate in order to be on line for the delay gate.

Delay combinations can be confusing for less experienced racers. When the delay is first introduced to this ability level, set the delay gate so as not to interfere with the line between the open gates. As racers become more experienced, the delay can be set in a more demanding way.

Giant Slalom Gate Combinations

A delay combination, as described previously, can also be set in a Giant Slalom course. Other gate combinations can be set, "but mainly on uninteresting terrain." (903.1.2) In Giant Slalom, any two poles of successive gates cannot be closer than ten meters apart.

Super-G Gate Combinations

"Gate combinations...are allowed only in small numbers. The distance between the successive turning poles can, in this case, be less than 25 meters, but must be at least 15 meters." (1003.1.2)

End of Course

Establish a rhythm with open gates to complete a course. Leave plenty of vertical distance between the last five to seven gates. At this point skiers may be tired; it is not the place to add required gate combinations. The last gate should direct the racers toward the middle of the finish line. The last gate should not be set too close to the finish.

Safety Precautions

Although not a responsibility of the course setter, it is important to be aware of precautions that must be taken to protect racers if they ski or slide off the course. Racers should be protected from obstacles by use of "high safety nets, safety fences, pads, straw in sacks, or similar appropriate means, if necessary together with slip-sheets. Unprotected, bound straw bales may not be used." (702.3)

Coaches should report to a jury member if they are unsatisfied with the course condition or the quality of protection provided alongside the course.

SELECTED RULES

Disqualification

A racer is disqualified (630) from the race if he/she:
  a. is late at the start or does not start.
  b. does not leave a Giant Slalom, Super-G, or Downhill start within five seconds before, or five seconds after the signal (word), "Go".
  c. does not leave a Slalom start within about 10 seconds of the command, "Go".
  d. "fails to cover the course on skis..." (630.1.7)
  e. does not finish the course on both skis, one ski, or with both feet when a fall occurs in the immediate finish area.
  f. misses a gate. Both of the competitor's ski tips and feet must cross the gate line between poles. "If a competitor loses a ski without committing a fault, e.g.: not by straddling a Slalom pole, then the tip of the remaining ski and both feet must have passed the gate line." (661.4.1) The racer should leave the course when a gate is missed or climb uphill to cross the gate line. In the latter case, as soon as the competitor's ski tips and boots cross uphill of the gate line, he/she can continue down the hill. He/she must clear the course if the next racer on the course approaches.
  g. "fails to give way to an overtaking competitor at the first call or interferes with his run" (630.1.9).

Interference

One situation race officials often have to deal with is the question of interference and the awarding of re-runs. Interference (623.2) occurs when the progress of the racer has been hindered by the:
  a. blocking of the course by an official, a spectator, an animal, or other hindrance.
  b. blocking of the course by a fallen competitor.
  c. objects in the course such as a lost ski pole or the ski of a previous competitor.
  d. absence of a gate knocked down by a previous competitor, and not promptly replaced.
  e. activities of first aid personnel.

When interference occurs the competitor must immediately ski off the course. "By continuing after interference, the competitor loses the right to claim a re-run." (631.1.3) The competitor or team captain must go to the nearest jury member to report what happened. If the jury feels the competitor was not interfered with, he/she could be disqualified.

Provisional Re-run

A provisional re-run is granted a competitor when the referee or a jury member cannot question the appropriate officials (gate officials, start or finish officials, for examples) in order to make a quick decision. Justification for the re-run must later be confirmed by the jury for it to be valid.

Protests

Protests (640) are submitted at the location designated on the official notice board, or at a location announced at the team captain's meeting. Protests, submitted in writing, can be made:

    a. against the course or its condition
    b. against disqualifications
    c. against timekeeping
    d. against another competitor or against an official

GLOSSARY

Aerodynamic: the position a skier assumes in order to cut through the air with the least amount of air resistance.

Angulation: creating lateral angles in the body that enhance balance. Angulation can occur in the knees and hips (in combination with flexing of these joints) and the spinal column.

Arc: the curved path of the ski in the snow.

Balancing point: a point on the foot that is located near the back of the arch, in front of the heel. Subtle fore and aft movements originating from this point allow skiers to adjust weight forward to start the turn, centered through the turn, and slightly back for the completion of the turn.

Balanced stance: the skier's center of mass (weight) lies in a vertical plane that is perpendicular to the skis and passes through the balancing point.

Banking: leaning inward (inclining toward the inside of the turn) with a relatively straight body position.

Carving: weighting and angulating the ski so that it bends into a circular arc, whereby the edge of the ski moves along a corresponding circular arc to form a sharp curved track in the snow. In pure carving, every point along the length of the ski follows the same path along the arc of the turn and there is no skidding.

Clearing poles: contact with Slalom flex poles to move them out of the way for a more direct line down a course. "Inside hand clear" and "outside hand clear" are two common methods for clearing poles.

Closed gate: the two poles of the gate are set vertically down a hill, along the fall line.

Come-from-behind: starting a turn after the rise line (from behind the turning pole) in order to complete the turn below the gate.

Corridor: two open gates that are set to designate one long turn in Super-G and Downhill events.

Countered position: the outside hip is slightly back in relation to the inside hip in a traverse or turn. Countering movements generally occur with angulation of the hip and spine.

Cross-block: term used for clearing poles by the "outside hand clear" method.

Cross-over transition: the skier's body crosses over the skis during the transition between turns.

Cross-under transition: the skier's legs quickly move laterally under the body during the transition between turns.

Curvilinear: a line or path that curves.

Delay combination: a gate combination consisting of an open gate, followed by a closed or oblique gate (the delay gate), followed by another open gate.

Disqualification: a breaking of rules that results in a racer's dismissal from a competition.

Dynamic: refers to the rapid adjustments of body position that the skier makes to stay in balance.

Edging: tipping of the ski onto one of its edges.

Edge angle: the amount a ski is tipped on edge. The edge angle is measured relative to a horizontal surface.

Exit angle: the direction of the skis when the racer goes by the turning pole. At this point, the turn should be completed and the skis already redirected in preparation for the upcoming turn.

Fall line: through any point on the hill, the fall line is the direction where the hill has the steepest slope. A snowball will roll in that direction.

Flex poles: poles that bend at the snow surface. Racers can move *flex* poles out of the way for a more direct line down a course, in comparison to the line set with *rigid* poles.

Flush: three or four closed gates set in a vertical combination.

Gate: two poles between which the racer must pass.

Gate line: the imaginary line between the *turning pole* and the outside pole of a gate.

Gliding: implies carved turns in which racers maximize speed by using the least amount of edge angle necessary to maintain their line through the gates.

Hairpin: two closed gates set in a vertical combination. The racer can enter a hairpin by skiing over (higher than) the top pole *(over-hairpin)*, or below the top pole *(into-hairpin)* of the first closed gate.

Hip angulation: an angle at the hip between the upper body and lower body. The upper body stays relatively vertical, with shoulders level, while the lower body is at a slant to the snow. This is a strong position because the skeletal alignment from the foot to the hip provides support.

Helper poles: markers or short-length poles that provide visual reference points for teaching tactics.

Inside ski: considering that a turn is part of a circle, the inside ski is closer to the center of the circle.

Interference: the progress of the racer has been hindered by a person or object that should not be on the course.

Javelin: an exercise in which the skier balances on the outside ski of the turn while the inside ski is lifted across the front of the outside ski. The placement of the inside ski encourages a countered position and makes it very difficult to rotate the outside hip through the turn.

Line: the skier's path down a race course.

Oblique gate: a gate that is set diagonally on a hill.

Open gate: a gate that is set horizontally across a hill, i.e., perpendicular to the fall line.

Outside Ski: considering that a turn is part of a circle, the outside ski is farther from the center of the circle.

Pivoting: twisting of a flat ski by rotating the foot about an axis perpendicular to the surface of the snow. The skier's direction of travel does not change.

Pre-jump: an action in which racers jump over abrupt changes of terrain and thereby minimize the negative effects of the terrain. Pre-jumps generally occur in Super-G or Downhill events.

Press: an action to keep the skis on the snow over a change of terrain. If flight occurs, this action assists the skier in assuming an aerodynamic tuck position through the air. Presses generally occur in Super-G or Downhill events.

Pressure control: adjustments a skier makes to control the location of the center of force acting on the skis. Weight transfer from ski to ski, fore/aft movements, and flexing/extending actions effect the amount and location of pressure on a ski.

Protest: a written objection, before or during a race, against the course or its condition, disqualifications, timekeeping, another competitor, or an official.

Provisional re-run: A second run is granted when the referee or a jury member cannot quickly decide if the competitor deserves another opportunity to race through a course. The jury must later decide whether to accept the re-run.

Racing Line: the racer's line through the course.

Radius: distance from the center of a circle to the edge of the circle. Slalom turns are generally considered to be short radius turns. Giant Slalom turns are medium radius turns. Super-G and Downhill turns are long radius turns.

Rise Line: an imagined line that extends uphill from the turning pole of each gate, and lies along the fall line. For all gates (open, closed, and oblique), turns should be started on or near the rise line.

Rotary Action: the action of turning or twisting the body along its vertical axis.

Safety Stop: pivoting of the skis into a sideslip and increasing edging to come to a stop.

Shinning: clearing of Slalom poles out of the way by contact with the shins.

Skidding: a combination of sliding, slipping and pivoting resulting in a turn.

Slipping: sideways travel of a flat ski.

Sliding: forward travel of a flat ski.

Speed Events: Super-G and Downhill.

Steering: an additional torque that is applied to change the path of the ski from the path of pure carving. The torque causes a pivoting action, such that steering always adds a skidding motion to the ski. Steering is applied to decrease the radius of an otherwise pure carved turn.

Stubby poles: flex poles, about two feet tall, that are used in drill courses. "Stubbies" allow skiers to ski close to a pole without having to clear the pole away with the upper body.

Synchronize: two or more skiers start and finish turns at the same time. Skiers can be in a horizontal, vertical or diagonal formation, or no fixed formation.

Tactics: the racer's line through the course. The term, *tactics*, can also apply to the racer's plan or strategy for skiing the course.

Technical Events: Slalom or Giant Slalom events.

Technique: how the formal elements of skiing are performed. Technique is usually evaluated by comparison with optimum body positions and ski positions for every type of maneuver encountered in freeskiing or racing. Optimum technique is a constantly evolving quality, subject to the current judgment of coaches, racers and skiing authorities.

Tuck: a compact, aerodynamic body position in which the back of the skier is essentially parallel to the surface of the skis.

Turning Pole: in a gate, the pole that is closer to the racer's curvilinear path.

Vertical Combinations: gate combinations consisting of closed gates. Hairpins and flushes are vertical combinations.

Yellow Zone: a designated location on a Downhill course at which racers are required to stop to avoid a dangerous situation located below that section. At a yellow zone, an official waves a yellow flag to signal the racer to come to a stop.

APPENDIX SKI HELMETS

Helmet technology has evolved tremendously in the past three years. Its development coincides, in a timely manner, to growth in the ski industry. Groomed slopes and high performance equipment allow skiers to reach high speeds. Obstacles such as snow-making machinery and lift towers are present. Ski slopes are often crowded, with skiers of different ages, skill levels, and speed capability sharing the same terrain. Even very young children participate in skiing.

Yet, many people are unaware of the protective and performance values of ski helmets. In other sports that involve speed, obstacles, collisions, and possible contact with stationary objects, protective head gear has evolved to be an accepted part of the athlete's equipment. Football, hockey, bicycling and in-line skating are examples. Helmets were not worn for these sports until technology evolved to make specific, practical head gear available. Now, helmets are widely used. Why is protective gear not as popular in skiing? Perhaps a reason is that our country, unlike some European countries, does not have a ski helmet standard at this time. There are no conclusive tests in the United States to prove that wearing helmets will reduce the risk of injury in skiing and snowboarding. "Certainly the Europeans are ahead of us for safety requirements for skiing." Dr. Warren Bowmen, National Medical Advisor for the *National Ski Patrol*, stated in a conversation concerning helmet standards in Europe. Some helmets that are available in the U.S. do meet European ski helmet standards. Helmets that meet these standards fulfill test requirements that are specific to the nature of skiing and snowboarding. The analysis does show that the helmets will provide added protection. Presently, the Boeri line of ski and snowboard helmets and the Briko line of ski helmets meet the "CEN" (European Committee for Standardization) ski helmet standard. This is a new standard which has been adopted by FIS Italy. Jofa helmets meet the ski helmet standard set forth by "The Swedish Board for Consumer Policies". Be wary that there may be helmets available that are marketed for skiing and stamped with a U.S. standard that is not specific toward skiing and snowboarding. It is important to note that helmets must be sized correctly and must also be the appropriate model for their intended use.

Helmets of the past were exclusive to Downhill racing, or borrowed from other sports such as motorcycling. Until recently, ski helmets designed for day-long wear were unavailable in the United States. Therefore, widespread use could not have occurred before this time. Perhaps now, a pattern similar to bicycling will develop: New bike technology allowed people to ride off-road on mountain bikes. Bike helmets evolved with the sport and became readily available to meet the demands of bicycling on variable terrain. Safety, performance and comfort were considered. People took advantage of this technology, and now, bicycle helmets are widely used by recreational cyclists. Now that ski helmet technology has matured, specific models are offered for every type of skier. Their availability makes it possible for everyone to take advantage of new safety and performance technology and consider the helmet option.

Is a preventive attitude necessary? Do helmets reduce the risk of injury? I asked Dr. Samuel W. Capra Jr. of the Incline Orthopaedic & Sports Medicine Clinic in Nevada, and he responded:

"I do not know of any definitive data currently in the medical literature on this subject. However, there is a significant amount of clinical data regarding children wearing helmets while bicycling.

Head injuries in children on bicycles account for two thirds of all bicycle related hospital admissions. Head injuries in children are also responsible for 85% of bicycle related deaths. It is estimated by a 1988 study in the American Journal of Sports Medicine, as well as a recent study in 1993 from the Southern Medical Journal, that helmet wearers have ten times less incidence of skull fractures in similar accidents than a helmetless bicyclist has.

For these reasons, I am strongly in favor of children wearing helmets while skiing. You have essentially the same conditions, where a child is going at a speed upwards of 20 mph and may potentially have a collision with either another, larger skier- or potentially with an immovable object such as a lift upright."

Someone who is well aware of the risk factors is Mimi Bodel, coordinator of Headsmart, a helmet safety program conducted by the National Head Injury Foundation (NHIF). "Head injury is the number one killer and disabler of young people in America," says Bodel. "Prevention is, at this time, the only cure for traumatic brain injury, and it will always be the best cure." The NHIF urges adults and children to be "headsmart," and always wear a helmet when doing any sport where the head is vulnerable.

Some people shy away from wearing a helmet because they envision the heavy Downhill helmets of years past. It wasn't always practical to wear a helmet all day long. Recent developments in technology have made helmets light-weight and comfortable to wear. New models are available for every discipline of skiing.

"Our goal in every model is to offer the highest level of protection possible without compromising performance and practicality. Weight, fit, hearing ability, and warmth are factors taken into consideration in the design." says Dennis Leedom of MPH Associates, the national distributor of Boeri ski helmets. Many helmets have a small opening at the ear so as not to interfere with hearing. Ski helmets also provide added warmth on cold weather days. The interior materials, combined with padding and plastic shell, make it unnecessary to wear a wool hat.

One popular concern is the question raised about obstructed vision, primarily peripheral vision. If you try on a helmet you will see that in no way does the edge of a helmet interfere with eye sight. Actually, it is the goggles, although necessary for eye protection, which can compromise sight.

Today's ski helmets attempt to maximize protection, comfort and performance. Dennis Leedom adds, "The evolution of today's specific ski helmet models give skiers valuable added protection that can make a difference. But few are aware that these helmets also have performance characteristics that will give you a higher level of confidence, excitement and enjoyment on the hill. Helmets reduce the effects of surrounding distractions like wind, cold and precipitation, helping you to focus on the terrain, snow conditions and your equipment." Some necessary features for all-day wear, Slalom, or Giant Slalom helmets include:

- a hard plastic shell that is shatter and puncture resistant, providing protection against sharp objects such as ski edges and immovable objects such as rocks and trees.
- an expanded polystyrene liner that partially absorbs the shock of an impact
- padding for a personalized, snug fit and for warmth
- an open ear design that does not disturb hearing or balance (a shorter shell version is now available in which the plastic shell does not cover the ear)
- an under-the-chin strap that positions the helmet properly and secures the fit

Optional features include:
- a padded rim for extra protection of the face
- jaw protection with a removable piece for added

protection of the face and teeth
- bright colors and graphics for high visibility. Small children become more visible to other skiers when they wear brightly colored helmets.

Super-G and Downhill helmets are constructed of kevlar and fiberglass shells for greater protection at high speeds.

When it comes to selecting a helmet, correct fit is just as crucial as necessary features. To ensure a secure fit, ski helmets should be worn without a hat underneath. The liner of the helmet provides the warmth of a hat. A helmet that is too large will not be as effective in preventing injury because the head can hit the inside of the helmet upon impact. For a child, a too large helmet can be too heavy.

Correct helmet size can be determined by measuring the head circumference (in inches or centimeters) and then referring to the manufacturer's sizing chart. Padding can be added to ensure a snug and comfortable fit. When an incorrectly sized helmet is excessively padded, protection is compromised, just as excessive padding in too large a ski boot hinders performance.

Helmet manufacturers now offer sizes ranging from very small helmets for children to adult XXL. Different models are designed to meet the needs of all-day wear and the demands of racing. A shorter shell design, similar in shape to a bike helmet with a sewn drop liner for warmth and comfort, is also available for all-day wear.

Helmets especially make sense for young skiers, and not only because they stand the greater chance of injury in a collision with an adult. Children are easily distracted and tend to be less aware than adults regarding changes in upcoming terrain and obstacles. Children's moves can be unpredictable, and it is common for them to dart across a busy slope to ski into the woods in search of adventure on a "tree trail."

In the ASTM (American Society for Testing and Materials) report on "Alpine Skiing Injuries in Children", printed in *Skiing Trauma and Safety: Ninth International Symposium*, a compilation of most common injury sites in a Swedish study group accounted head injuries at 14%. The text states,

"Only a small percentage of children under 10 suffered head injuries in contrast to children 10 to 14 years of age and adolescents. This is probably due to the common use of protective helmets by the youngest children, and older children and adolescents ought to wear protective helmets as well."

Some people are concerned that helmets for small children actually increase the chance of neck injury in an impact because of the additional weight. This could be true if the child is skiing in a helmet that is not made specifically for skiing, for example a motorcycle helmet, or if the child is using an inappropriate ski helmet model such as a Downhill racing helmet. Of course, the child should not wear a helmet that is too large, and therefore too heavy. As stated before, correct fit is essential for optimal head protection.

Helmet technology has taken huge strides over the past three years. Now, a full range of sizes is available, and there are different models to choose from. The ultimate decision to wear a ski helmet, however, lies with the individual skier or parent. As Dennis Leedom suggests, "The best way to decide is to select the appropriate model and try for yourself."

BIBLIOGRAPHY

Abraham, Horst. *Teaching Concepts ATM*, Professional Ski Instructors of America.

Foster, Ellen Post. *Alpine Skills Achievement Manual*, Turning Point Ski Foundation.

Foster, Ellen Post. *Alpine Star*, Volume 10, Issue 1, United States Skiing, Youth Ski League, Park City, UT.

Foster, Ellen Post. *Conditioning Skills for Alpine Skiing*, Turning Point Ski Foundation.

The International Ski Competition Rules, (International Ski Federation rule book) Edition 1992.

Alpine Skills Achievement Manual and Conditioning Skills for Alpine Skiing are available from the Turning Point Ski Foundation, PO Box 943, Edwards, CO 81632

The production of this book was made possible through generous contributions from *Skis Dynastar, Lange boots, MPH Associates, Inc.* (distributors of *Boeri* ski helmets), *Arapahoe Basin Resort*, and the *Turning Point Ski Foundation*. In addition, a grant was provided by the *PSIA-RM* division's *Education Foundation*. Other equipment was provided by *Goode* poles and *Marker USA* bindings. Clothing was provided by *Spyder Active Sports*.